KINGSTON'S PAST RE-DISCOVERED

I. St. Mary's chapel, Kingston by an unknown artist, possibly of the late seventeenth century. The chapel was not rebuilt after its collapse in 1728, but its site was carefully excavated by Alderman Finny in 1926. (**KHC** file print K1-1812).

KINGSTON'S PAST REDISCOVERED

by

Joan Wakeford

(Edited by Paul Hodges*)*

Published by

PHILLIMORE

for

KINGSTON UPON THAMES
ARCHAEOLOGICAL SOCIETY

and

SURREY LOCAL HISTORY COUNCIL

1990

1990
Published by
PHILLIMORE & CO. LTD.
Shopwyke Hall,
Chichester, Sussex, England

for
KINGSTON UPON THAMES ARCHAEOLOGICAL SOCIETY
and
SURREY LOCAL HISTORY COUNCIL
Guildford, Surrey

as extra volume number three of
Surrey History

 K.U.T.A.S. 1990

ISBN 0 85033 770 4

Printed and bound in Great Britain by
Biddles Ltd, Guildford and King's Lynn

Cover Illustration: THE REAR OF THE OLD COURT HALL. See plate XXVI for description.

CONTENTS

II. The old timber bridge across the Thames, 1829. The artist has worked from the Hampton Wick bank, upstream of his subject and in the shadow of its stone replacement, part of which can be seen on the extreme right. (**KHC** file print K1-508).

J.E. WAKEFORD

AN APPRECIATION BY THE PRESIDENT OF K.U.T.A.S.

Joan Wakeford was a founder member of Kingston upon Thames Archaeological Society, and although I did not meet her myself until we moved to Surrey, her reputation had gone before her. Robin Kenward had spoken of her as one of her most interesting students and a tower of strength in K.U.T.A.S. After I took over Robin's courses and joined the Society, I soon experienced Joan's quality myself. As soon as it was known that a building in Kingston was threatened or a site was to be excavated, Joan was working on the documentation and finding valuable and interesting information.

As a member of my lecture groups she was equally helpful, telling us relevant facts about early Kingston and its documentation. She fascinated us with her knowledge. She teased me that she was not interested in archaeology and only came to my lectures to hear what I was going to say! Nevertheless she was rarely absent, and for one who professed not to be interested in archaeology she was a remarkably faithful member of our society, a regular attender at meetings and a provider of wise counsel. Once, when we had a morning class, she confessed that she could not join it because she often worked far into the night and could never undertake to be anywhere at 10 in the morning.

Joan was a very private person but always ready to respond to others and many members of K.U.T.A.S. counted her a friend and have felt her loss deeply.

During her lifetime it had been suggested that a collection of her papers on topics related to Kingston should be published but, a true scholar, she was dissatisfied with their quality and wanted to revise them. Sadly she did not live to do this. Although it is against her own wishes, members of K.U.T.A.S. and many others will be glad that it has been decided to publish this volume of her papers, albeit unrevised by their author, as a memorial to her invaluable work and service.

Elizabeth S. Eames, M.B.E., F.S.A.,

President.

EDITORIAL INTRODUCTION

K.U.T.A.S. decided to ask Surrey Local History Council to help them to publish Miss Wakeford's papers in their unrevised form, despite the declared reservations of the author, for three main reasons. First, it believes that this is the most appropriate way of acknowledging the substantial contribution made by Miss Wakeford to the work of the Society over many years. Secondly, it considers that Miss Wakeford's research achievements deserve a more permanent public memorial than she herself was inclined to seek. Thirdly, and most importantly, it believes that even in their unrevised state, the papers make a major addition to our knowledge and understanding of the town's past, and contain much that is of permanent value. At the same time, the Society wishes to keep faith with the author by impressing upon readers the need to regard the papers in the same light as Miss Wakeford herself. They should not be read as definitive accounts, but as interim, and in some cases initial statements whose chief purpose is to highlight interesting local issues and to generate further research and discussion. Nor should it be assumed that the papers necessarily provide an accurate guide to Miss Wakeford's views at the time of her death, for inevitably her fertile mind ran ahead of what she had committed to paper.

Joan Wakeford was a gifted and imaginative local historian. Her main interests were the topographical development of Kingston and the history of its individual buildings. She was essentially what some have called 'a landscape historian'. The focus of her work was in part deliberately chosen, but also to some extent an accidental consequence of the role that she came to play in K.U.T.A.S. during the '70s and '80s. Her topographical research was often done in response to the needs of the Society's practicing archaeologists. It was motivated by a conviction that excavation would not be worthwhile unless it encompassed the integration of evidence from the soil with written sources, and the formulation of conclusions consistent with both. She researched particular sites and areas of the town as they became available for archaeological investigation, and also sought to establish an overall framework for local archaeology by identifying fundamental problems concerning the origins and early growth of Kingston for which the documentation is inadequate, and where progress in understanding will come, if at all, only through excavation. In the same way her work on local buildings was also intended to advance the Society's programme, in this case its commitment to the study and recording of Kingston's dwindling architectural heritage. Again she believed that an historical perspective was essential if experts in another discipline - in this case the interpretation of vernacular architecture - were to make the most effective use of their skills. Some of her papers were prompted by threats of redevelopment, others by private enquiries from property owners, and many reflect the successful working relationship based on a shared identity of purpose that she established with Mr. I. J. West, the Society's leading authority on local vernacular architecture. To the extent that archaeologists, local historians and students of vernacular architecture now take the virtues of inter-disciplinary cooperation as read, Miss Wakeford's work for K.U.T.A.S. has inevitably lost some of its pioneering edge. But when the Society was formed the barriers between the disciplines were still largely intact, and thus she deserves to be remembered as an advocate and practitioner of what for the time was very much an innovatory approach to local study.

Miss Wakeford's work shows a consistent attempt to bring to bear on the study of Kingston's past the fruits of modern academic thinking about the nature of landscape research, particularly as it has matured at the University of Leicester Department of English Local History under Professor Hoskins and his successors. Her stress on inter-disciplinary cooperation to which attention has just been drawn is one clear sign of this. Others are her concern to extend the scope of study beyond the traditional and elitist preoccupation with Kingston's royal associations and presumed role in national history; the healthy scepticism with which she treats long-cherished myths about the town's early development; and her understanding of the landscape, whether in the form of street names, boundaries or other physical components, as a subtle and complex record of the interaction of human settlers with their natural environment over many centuries. There is no obvious precedent for this among existing studies of Kingston, and on these grounds alone Miss Wakeford can claim to have made an original contribution to local knowledge and understanding.

Another important feature of Miss Wakeford's work is her effective use of documentary sources. Over the years she acquired an unrivalled knowledge of the Kingston Borough archives and of Kingston material in the Surrey Record Office, both in terms of content and of the particular circumstances in which individual classes of record were conceived. To the extent that her papers offer a sustained and informed commentary upon this material, they rank above most of what has hitherto been written about the town. She also trawled more distant waters, including the British Library, the Minet Library, the Public Record Office, the Bodleian and the National Library of Wales. Consequently, her papers, together with her copious working notes (now deposited in the Kingston Borough archives under the reference numbers KX72 and KX79) provide a comprehensive guide to the range of surviving sources for Kingston's past which will be immensely valuable to future researchers. In her handling of sources Miss Wakeford also improved significantly upon the past. Though sometimes lapsing into a traditional narrative approach (the tendency is perhaps exaggerated by the note form in which some papers survive), her writing is generally more critical and discriminating than Kingston's earlier historians. Sources are integrated more effectively within the text, providing an initial stimulus to discussion as well as determining its subsequent shape and direction. They are analysed more carefully and with greater regard for ambiguity and anachronism. They are used more consistently and vigorously to evaluate received wisdom as represented by the town's antiquarian 'authorities'. The quality of her treatment is also enhanced by a lively historical imagination, most clearly seen in the subtle inferences extracted from seemingly dry and uninformative factual detail, in the relationships established between scattered fragments of information (thus showing them to be parts of a common pattern) and in the judgements made on the basis of apparently unremarkable topographical features. Yet imaginative insight is always tempered by respect for the force of rational argument, so that the basic intellectual integrity of the writing is never compromised by wild flights of historical fantasy.

Miss Wakeford's papers are too specialised in focus and content to constitute an 'History' of Kingston in the generally accepted sense of the term. Nevertheless, they still contribute significantly to our perceptions of the wider canvas of the town's past. General ideas occasionally appear, especially in the topographical items: the image of Kingston as an island settlement is an obvious example, and others are the notion of the town as part of a more complex local structure including two other administrative nuclei (Norbiton and Surbiton), and the suggestion that the establishment of the medieval settlement brought to an end a long sequence of local migration whose earlier focal points included Coombe Hill and what later became the manor of Kingston-Canbury. Running through the papers, too, is an appreciation of themes and issues that would need to be addressed in a full history of the medieval and early-modern town. These include local government (in particular the interrelationship of formal powers as conveyed by royal charter and the practical administration of the town as revealed by Corporation records); economic growth (especially the development of important local industries such as milling and brewing); and social structure (notably the effects on this of such diverse influences as the confiscation and redistribution of religious property at the time of the Dissolution, the practice of land purchase by wealthy London merchants and the annual migration to Hampton Court of the royal household during the sixteenth and seventeenth centuries). These and other more specialised matters are rarely addressed in a direct way - indeed, some appear implicitly rather than explicitly - but they occur sufficiently often to suggest that in private Miss Wakeford was a fertile and imaginative thinker about the local community in the round, and that over the years she formed a clear mental picture of the more salient features of the town's general historical evolution. It can only be regretted that she lacked the time and inclination to delineate this picture in a more permanent and detailed form.

Though occasionally lacking polish (a consequence no doubt of the fact that they were not originally intended for publication) Miss Wakeford's papers demonstrate an underlying concern for professional standards of historical research. This is the more remarkable given that she came to the study of Kingston's past after a career in legal administration, and therefore without the benefit of sustained formal training in the discipline of history. In later life she successfully obtained the University of London Extra-Mural Diploma in History, and also deepened her general historical knowledge by attending short courses, conferences and other professiomal gatherings. But for all this she was largely self-taught, and her status as a local historian, as she herself often pointed out, always remained that of an enthusiastic amateur. Few amateurs, and certainly none of those who have worked on Kingston, have dignified their status with such 'professional' awareness.

In editing Miss Wakeford's papers, the guiding principle of policy has been the need to mould them into a coherent and effective publication while preserving the spirit and integrity of the writing. To this end they have been arranged in two parts, each reflecting a major focus of her research interests; and within each part, chronologically on the basis of content rather than date of composition. Editorial changes to the original form and content of the papers have been kept to a minimum. The main organisational changes include the introduction of a uniform referencing system for footnotes; the integration within some papers of supplementary notes separately written by Miss Wakeford as correctives to her earlier work; and the amalgamation of discrete but thematically related items to form balanced 'chapters'. With one exception, textual alterations are limited to the addition of occasional headings and subheadings, some extra footnotes (the originals are uneven in this respect) and the provision of short introductory paragraphs identifying the dates of composition, locating the originals and defining more precisely the special interest and importance of each item. The exception concerns a small number of papers surviving only in note form: here, for obvious reasons, the degree of editorial imput has necessarily been greater. Major modifications, both organisational and textual, are explained in the footnotes and indicated by the use of squared brackets. The illustrations accompanying the text (also an editorial addition) have been selected to complement the message of Miss Wakeford's writing and in the light of her own long-standing interest in the pictorial evidence for Kingston's past. A sketch-map has been added to assist readers unfamiliar with the local landscape.

Paul Hodges

Kingston upon Thames Archaeological Society
& Roehampton Institute
Spring 1990.

ACKNOWLEDGEMENTS

Miss Wakeford's footnotes show that she was always careful to give credit to those who had helped her at appropriate points in her text, but she would also no doubt have wished for a general acknowledgement of assistance received. Among those to whom she was indebted at many points in her work were Mr. I. J. West (especially for expert guidance on local domestic architecture); Mrs. A. McCormack and Mrs. M. Vaughan-Lewis (respectively present and former Kingston Borough Archivists); Dr. D. Robinson (Surrey County Archivist) and his staff at the Surrey Record Office; Mrs. M. Shipley (Borough Heritage Officer) and her colleagues at the Kingston Heritage Centre; and Miss J. Sampson of the *Surrey Comet*. Valuable assistance on particular problems was also given by Mr. J. W. Cross; Dr. A. Taylor; Mr. L. Wallis; Mr. A. W. E. Valler; and the staffs of the Society of Friends Library, the British Library, the Public Record Office (Chancery Lane section) and the Bodleian Library.

My task as editor was greatly facilitated by the help of many of those already mentioned; in particular, Mrs. A. McCormack and the staffs of the Surrey Record Office and the Kingston Heritage Centre. To these should be added the names of Miss C. Dimmer and Mr. L. Green, who with Mrs. McCormack joined me in forming the small working party of K.U.T.A.S. that took general responsibility, for this publication on behalf of the full committee of the society; Mrs. Laurette Burton who patiently transferred, the final text to the word processor; Mr. D. Hastie who kindly prepared the maps; and Mr. K. Gravett who gave expert and valuable advice on publication, and who single-handedly prepared, the proofs. Finally, I should like to acknowledge the support of the committee of K.U.T.A.S. which on behalf of the society gave unstinting encouragement, both moral and financial, to the production of this memorial volume.

All those involved in production are grateful to the following for permission to reproduce the illustrations contained in this volume: the Surrey Record Office; the Kingston Heritage Centre; the British Library; the *Surrey Comet*.

ABBREVIATIONS

Note:

The footnotes have been placed at the end of each chapter, rather than at the bottom of each page. Miss Wakeford's original footnotes vary considerably in form and frequency. To achieve consistency they have been recast to fit a uniform referencing scheme based on abbreviations, as tabulated below. Additional footnotes are enclosed within square brackets.

Abbreviations:

Apprentices	*Kingston upon Thames Register of Apprentices 1563-1713,* ed. A. Daly, (**SRS** vol. 28, 1974).
ASC	*Anglo-Saxon Chronicle,* ed. D. Whitelock with D. C. Douglas & S. I. Tucker, (1961).
Aubrey	J. Aubrey, *Natural history and antiquities of the County of Surrey,* (1718-9, reprinted with introduction by J. L. Nevinson, 1975). All references are to the reprint.
Ayliffe	G. W. Ayliffe, *Old Kingston: Recollections of an Octogenarian,* (1914, with facsimile reprint in 1972). All references are to the reprint.
Biden	W. D. Biden, *The History and Antiquities of the Ancient and Royal Town of Kingston-upon-Thames,* (1852).
BL	British Library.
Brayley	E. W. Brayley, *A History of Surrey,* 5 vols., (1841).
Britannia	*Camden's Britannia: Surrey & Sussex,* ed. G. J. Copley, (1977).
CIPM	*Calendar of Inquisitions Post Mortem,* (1898 etc.).
CPR	*Calendar of Patent Rolls. . .* (1891 etc.).
DBRG(S)	Domestic Buildings Research Group (Surrey).
DBSurrey	*Domesday Book: Surrey,* ed. J. Morris, (Phillimore's History from the Sources series, 1975). References follow the distinctive numbering scheme of this edition.
DNB	*Dictionary of National Biography,* 66 vols., (1885 etc.).
EPNS	English Place-Names Society.
GM	Gentleman's Magazine.
Heales	A. Heales, *The Early History of the church of Kingston-upon-Thames, together with the history of the Free Chapel of St. Mary Magdalene, Kingston. . .* (1883).
KBR	Kingston Borough Records.
KHC	Kingston Heritage Centre.

KPR(B,M,Bu)	Kingston upon Thames Parish Registers (Baptism, Marriage, Burial). The originals are in **SRO** P33/1, transcripts of early volumes in **KHC.**
KUTAS BULLETIN /CHRONICLE /NL	*Kingston upon Thames Archaeological Society Bulletin/ Chronicle/ Newsletter* (August 1969, etc.). Early booklets (to November 1970) were called *Bulletin* and numbered consecutively. *Chronicle* was adopted in January 1971, but booklets were now distinguished only by date (month and year). *Newsletter* was introduced in 1977 with consecutive numbering reappearing a little later.
Leland	J. Leland, *Itinerary in England and Wales in or about the years 1535-1543,* ed. L. Toulmin Smith, (5 vols. 1964).
M&B	O. Manning & W. Bray, *History and Antiquities of the County of Surrey,* (3 vols. 1804, 1809, 1814).
M&B(Percival)	*The History and Topography of the County of Surrey. . . commenced by O. Manning. . . continued and enlarged by W. Bray. . . illustrated with upwards of 6000 drawings, prints, maps and plans,* (30 vols. 1847). This is a grangerized version of **M&B**, privately produced for Richard Percival of Highbury Park, Islington, and is now in the **BL.**
Merryweather	F. S. Merryweather, *Half a Century of Kingston History,* (1887).
Merton Records	*The Records of Merton Priory,* ed. A. Heales, (1898) .
Pevsner	B. Cherry & N. Pevsner, *The Buildings of England: London 2, South* (1983).
Pevsner,Surrey	I. Nairn & N. Pevsner, *The Buildings of England: Surrey,* (2nd. edn., revised B. Cherry, 1971).
PNSurrey	*The Place-Names of Surrey,* ed. J. E. B. Gover, A. Mawer & F. M. Stenton, (**EPNS** vol XI, 1934) .
PRO	Public Record Office. All references are to documents at Chancery Lane.
SAC	*Surrey Archaeological Collections,* (1858 etc.).
Sampson	J. Sampson, *The Story of Kingston,* (1972).
SAS(Bull)	*Surrey Archaeological Society Bulletin.*
SC	*Surrey Comet.* Back numbers are available on microfilm in **KHC.**
SRO	Surrey Record Office.
SRS	Surrey Record Society.
VCHSurrey	*Victoria History of the Counties of England: Surrey,* ed. H. E. Malden, (4 vols. 1902-12).

Of the maps frequently mentioned in the text, only the Tithe Map (**SRO** P33/2/1), of 1840, is consistently footnoted. Copies of other maps - Rocque's 1745 map of London and its Environs, Hornor's 1813 plan of Kingston and the various editions of the Ordnance Survey maps - are available in **SRO** and **KHC.**

J. E. WAKEFORD: ADDITIONAL WRITINGS

In addition to the essays published in this volume, Miss Wakeford's written work included the following contributions:

1956/57   *The Administration of Kingston upon Thames, Surrey in the early eighteenth century*, (unpublished study submitted for the University of London Extra-Mural Diploma in History).

1973   *Archaeology and Development in Kingston upon Thames*, (KUTAS NL, June 1973) - contributor with other members of the Society.

1977   'Kingston upon Thames, 2A St. James' Rd - an eighteenth-century Counting House', SAC, vol. 71 (1977), pp. 255-257 - written with I. J. West.

1979   *Picton House and the People connected with it*, (KUTAS Occasional Paper No. 2) - contributor with other members of the Society.

      'Notes on the early history of Coombe', Appendix 3 to L. E. Gent, *The Manor of Coombe or Coombe Nevill*, (KUTAS Occasional Paper No. 3) -- Miss Wakeford also saw this work to press after Mr. Gent's death.

      Site of St. Luke's Church and School, Kingston, (unpublished typescript in KHC).

1980   'The Horsefair Development', KUTAS NL 5 (March), pp. 3-5.

1984   'Two *walh* names in the fields of Kingston', SAC, vol. 74, (1984), pp. 251-256.

1985   'The royal portraits formerly at Kingston upon Thames', SAC, vol. 76, (1985), pp. 109-113.

1986   'Old Mill House, 179 Villiers Rd., Kingston', KUTAS NL 24 (February, 1986) -- written with Mr. I. J. West.

      'News from Kingston upon Thames', KUTAS NL 25 (June, 1986).

      'News from Kingston upon Thames', KUTAS NL 26 (November, 1986).

For Miss Wakeford's working notes, see KBR KX72; KX79.

LIST OF ILLUSTRATIONS

PRESENTATION COPIES

1. *The Worshipful the Mayor of the Royal Borough of Kingston upon Thames*

2. Freda Sharp
3. Phillipa Crouch
4. Anne Murray, *Lady Murray of Gravesend*
   (The three sisters of the late Author).

SUBSCRIPTION LIST

5. Elizabeth Eames, *President of K.U.T.A.S.*

6. Anne Baker
7. Paul Barnfield
8. Ann Bott
9. Wendy and John Boult
10. *The late* Audrey Collyer
11. Douglas Colpus
12. Graeme Cranch
13. Carol Dimmer
14. Julian French
15. Nora Gent
16. Margaret Gerrish
17. Leslie Green
18. Edith and Fred Hastings
19. Paul Hodges
20. Philippa Hussey
21. David Jones
22. Robin Kenward
23. Joyce Little
24. Monica Lunn
25. Angela Lysons
26. Anne and Jeff McCormack
27. Pat McKenna
28. Martin Morris
29. Peggy Morris
30. John Musty
31. Steve Nelson
32. Margaret Nobbs
33. Diana O'Connor
34. Margaret Potten
35. John Pulford
36. Joan Ruddle
37. June Sampson
38. Marion Shipley
39. Patricia and Tony Smith
40. Elizabeth Stazicker
41. Richard Taylor
42. Maggie Vaughan-Lewis
43. Heather and Henry Vit
44. Richard Watson
45. Ian West
46. Julie Wileman
47. Lewis Yates

xix

SKETCH MAP OF KINGSTON
SHOWING THE MAIN BUIILDINGS MENTIONED IN THE TEXT

SOME FORMER STREET NAMES:

Barreway or Bar(r)e Lane	now *Lower Ham Road.*
Canbury Lane	now *Richmond Road.*
Cooks Row	now *Market Place, East side.*
Felders or Velders Lane	now *Fairfield Road.*
Gigg Hill	now *Eden Street (Market Place end).*
Heathen Street	now *Eden Street.*
Hoggestreet	now *Brook Street.*
King Street	now *Church Street/Clarence Street (west end).*
Norbiton Street	now *Clarence Street/London Road.*
Oil Mill Lane	now *Villiers Road.*
West-by-Thames	now *High Street.*

Note: No attempt has been made to show the recent (1988-89) road alterations in central Kingston.

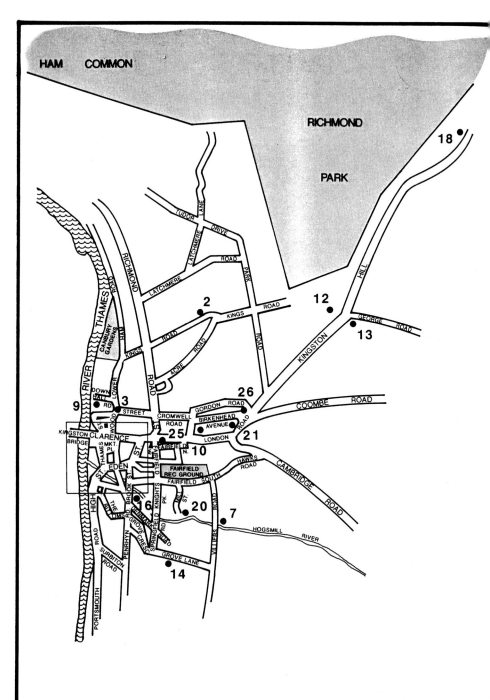

HAM COMMON

RICHMOND

PARK

18

TUDOR DRIVE

LATCHMERE LANE

LATCHMERE ROAD

PARK ROAD

RICHMOND ROAD

LATCHMERE ROAD

2

KINGS ROAD

12

KINGSTON HILL

GEORGE ROAD

13

CANBURY GARDENS

KINGS ROAD

KINGS ROAD

ACRE ROAD

THAMES

RIVER

26

LOWER

DOWN HALL RD.

9

3

STREET

GORDON ROAD

CROMWELL ROAD

BIRKENHEAD AVENUE

COOMBE ROAD

KINGSTON CLARENCE

25

21

BRIDGE

MKT. PL.

FAIRFIELD N.

LONDON ROAD

10

THAMES ST.

FAIRFIELD W.

EDEN

FAIRFIELD REC GROUND

HAWKS ROAD

CAMBRIDGE ROAD

FAIRFIELD SOUTH

HIGH

THE BITTOMS

BROOKS ST.

KNIGHTS PK.

16

PENRHYN RD.

GROVE CRESC.

SPRINGFIELD RD.

20

VILLIERS ROAD

7

ROAD

SURBITON ROAD

GROVE LANE

HOGSMILL RIVER

PORTSMOUTH

14

© D.H. 1989.

KEY

1. All Saints' Parish Church.
2. The Barracks, King's Road (site of).
3. Barre Bridge (approximate site of).
4. Bishops Hall (site of).
5. Bridewell Prison (site of).
6. Bridge (line of earlier structure).
7. Chapel/Oil Mill (site of) and Old Mill House.
8. Court/Market Hall (site of earlier structure).
9. Downhall (site of).
10. Elmfield, London Road.
11. Folly/Prison House (site of).
12. Gallows (approximate site of).
13. George & Dragon (formerly the Fox and Coney), Kingston Hill.
14. Grove Lodge/Farm.
15. Hercombe Place (site of).
16. Hogg's Mill (site of).
17. King John's Dairy (site of).
18. Kingston Hill Place.
19. La Ryole/Ryall Farm (approximate site of).
20. Middle Mill (site of).
21. Norbiton Place (site of).
22. Old Crown (formerly the Checker), Church Street.
23. Rowbarge, Old Bridge Street (site of).
24. Stonebridge (approximate site of).
25. Three Coneys, London Road.
26. Workhouse, Nos. 155/157 London Road (site of).

THE TOWN CENTRE

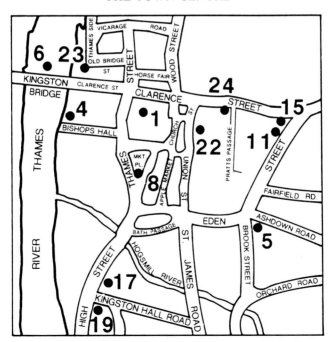

PART I:

STUDIES IN THE TOPOGRAPHY
OF KINGSTON

III. The Horse Fair c.1895, looking west towards the junction with Thames Street. These buildings, together with much of the surrounding area, were cleared soon after the photograph was taken. (**KHC** file print K1-3880)

IV. A slum cottage near Marsh's mill in Water Lane at the end of the nineteenth century. Behind this building, less than a stone's throw away, lay the meadows and orchards of Down Hall. (**SC** 20C 639).

I

SOME THOUGHTS ON THE ORIGINS OF KINGSTON UPON THAMES

[This opening paper combines two separate but clearly related items found among Miss Wakeford's working notes: an undated draft on the development of the Kingston area in Romano-British and early Saxon times (evidently written as an introduction to a projected but never completed 'History of Kingston') and a series of notes entitled 'Kingston: some caveats on the early history', drafted in 1980 {1}. Over the years Miss Wakeford evidently thought a good deal about the broader canvas of Kingston's past, and this paper provides a valuable record of her conclusions regarding the town's more distant history. Of special interest is the way in which it calls into question Victorian accounts of the town by challenging the traditional emphasis on Kingston's royal associations. It also raises a number of important issues that are explored more fully in subsequent papers, and is thus an ideal introduction to the collection.]

In recent years there has been an interest in the past of Kingston upon Thames not seen since the early years of Queen Victoria's reign. Redevelopment has given opportunities for archaeological excavation and earlier work has been studied and reinterpreted with the aid of modern techniques and greater knowledge of history and pre-history. Documents not readily accessible to our predecessors are adding to our picture of the local scene and a truer appreciation of the passage of distant time now forms part of our cultural background. Much work remains to be done (the sources of local history are truly inexhaustible) but perhaps it is now time for an interim account of the early growth of the local community in order to bring forward some aspects suggested by recent work and perhaps in the process to bury some earlier misconceptions. In particular, I think we need to look again, and in a much more critical way, at Kingston's much vaunted royal associations. Every community has its own importance and for those who live among acres of fairly new buildings to feel that their town had deep roots in the past is a valuable factor in its life. But it is not necessary to assert a higher status for that town than for others, or to be continually searching for evidence that it came to royal or national notice at particular times, for that is only a sophisticated form of the common claim 'Queen Elizabeth slept here' ! {2}. To earlier historians of Kingston the temptation was especially strong because the inauguration here of several of the later Anglo-Saxon kings was recorded {3}. Whether these events were the cause or the consequence of the development of Kingston, or even merely incidental to it, they cannot justify a frantic search for continuing royal connections to the exclusion of the many factors which must have been of more importance to local people: nor should they lead us to make unwarranted presumptions about the importance of Kingston in pre-Conquest times. Before the establishment of local Record Offices, the archives available for research were predominantly the records of central government and historians had difficulty in setting them in a local context. To a certain extent the earlier research can now be reassessed, but the vastly increased quantity of documents and the realisation that many other types of information are also relevant to the study of local history have made research more onerous. For that reason (among others) the present account can be only a tentative sketch of what should eventually be possible.

Romano-British Times

Nineteenth-century archaeological discoveries in the Kingston area may have been significant, but are now difficult to date or locate precisely: and moreover, the written reports made at the time are often compromised by the Victorian urge to prove that Kingston was the place where Caesar crossed the Thames on the first Roman expedition into Britain. As Caesar did not indicate that any settlement existed at the crossing place, the question of its precise location is arguably not as interesting or important as has sometimes been thought: suffice it to say that the Thames must have been fordable in many places in early times, and that the tracks which must have led to these fords have long been overshadowed by the military roads later built by the Romans themselves. But though the old reports of Romano-British finds can usually not be related to precise places, it none the less seems clear that the most important general area for them was on the high land in the Kingston Hill area. In one case, however, a brooch illustrated by Biden has been associated with a report of burials discovered in the 1820s near the Thames on the site of the later Canbury gas-works {4}. Other indications of Romano-British presence near the river downstream from the present town have come to light on the site of the Electricity Works in Down Hall Road, and more recently near Canbury Passage {5}. The Anglo-Saxons gave the name Walehull to a part of the same area, and this indicates its use by the people who were there before the Saxons arrived. They also called land on the slopes of Kingston Hill Waleport, and this suggests that they could see there some evidence that it was, or had been the site of a British town {6}. As late as the sixteenth century, Leland reported that remains of buildings still appeared on the slopes of the hill during ploughing and digging {7}. But whilst there may have been a fairly substantial Romano-British presence at several points in the Kingston area (though not, it would seem, within the central sector of the present town), there is nothing to support Biden's confident statement that Claudius had built a 'substantial wooden bridge' here. This is based on Thomas Gale's early eighteenth-century commentary on the well-known Antonine Itinerary, though the source from which Gale himself drew the idea is not recorded. An earlier commentary on the Itinerary by William Burton, master of the Free Grammar School at Kingston, does not suggest a Roman bridge here, and Manning, writing in the early nineteenth century, remarked that he knew of no authority for Gale's view {8}.

2

The Early Saxon Period

We no longer think that the Saxons arrived suddenly in Britain after the departure of the Roman armies, bringing fire and sword and chasing the Britons westwards to Wales. The English colonisation took a long time and place-name evidence (e.g. the Walehull/Waleport names above) suggests that Anglo-Saxon and British settlements must have existed side by side in parts of south-eastern England. Nothing is known about the progress of the Saxon settlement in the Kingston locality, though one or two general suggestions can be made about what happened in Surrey as a whole. In the first place, it must be remembered that the Saxons did not establish a single English state in these early centuries, but many kingdoms of various sizes, some quite possibly taking over existing areas of local jurisdiction: nor must we forget that these were likely to change their individual status from time to time through military defeats, failure of heirs or local power politics {9}. The earliest documents which mention Surrey (which was not, of course, necessarily identical with the later administrative county) are connected with the endowment of the monastery of Chertsey {10}. As the monastery is stated to have been founded by Egbert, king of Kent in 666, it may well be that at that time Kentish authority extended over this area. However, when further endowments of land on the southern side of the Thames between Chertsey and Molesey were added by a charter of *c*.672 (now thought to be substantially authentic), the donor, Frithewald, styled *provinciae Surrianoru subregulus,* was evidently a subordinate of Wulfhere, ruler of the Midland kingdom of Mercia, then in the process of extending its influence southwards {11}. The names of Surrey and Chertsey both occur in Bede and hint at something of their early history {12}. Bede refers to *Certotaesei* or *Ceroti insula,* indicating the place was then an island on the Thames, and had belonged, probably within the knowledge of the Anglo-Saxons, to a man with a British name {13}. And just as Frithewald in his charter referred to the 'province' of the men of Surrey, Bede calls Surrey a *regio* or district, and his form of the name of Surrey contains an element 'ge' which also means 'district'. This element occurs in the early forms of other English place-names and is now regarded as denoting an area of jurisdiction {14}. As the whole name means 'the southern district', it suggests that earlier in the Saxon settlement it had been associated with another area north of the Thames, presumably Middlesex, rather than with Kent. But by the time of the Chertsey foundation, Middlesex had become part of the East-Saxon kingdom.

Archaeological excavation in the Kingston area has so far produced little evidence of early Anglo-Saxon settlement, but the fact that so much of the area was developed or redeveloped in the nineteenth century when such evidence would not have been recognised may partly account for this. Also, as the part first settled is traditionally believed to have been on level ground much subject to floods (downstream of the old Kingston bridge), dating evidence may have been carried away or covered by the later course of the river {15}. In particular there is a complete absence of Anglo-Saxon pre-Christian burials (or indeed of any burial grounds other than that of the parish church of All Saints). It is worth remembering that until very recently there were almost no archaeological remains of Anglo-Saxon London, though it undoubtedly existed. London was, of course, a special case, and it is not

3

likely that any early Saxon settlement in the neighbourhood of Kingston had any urban characteristics: but at least we may say that it would be premature to assume that nothing remains to be found. At the same time it would be naive to set our hopes too high, since the place where the earlier river crossing was is said to have been called Moreford, an old English word meaning 'marshy ford', which suggests that it was the ford (rather than any settlement) which was the most noticeable feature {16}. The marshy character of the area reflected in the name may have been a consequence of the deterioration in the climate in the later Romano-British and sub-Roman periods, when the level of the Thames rose, as for example at Brentford.

Late-Saxon Times

The name Kingston is of Saxon origin and there are at least twenty-four surviving examples, all given the meaning 'King's tun: royal manor' {17}. The earliest documentary reference to our Kingston is usually assumed to date from 838 when a synod was held in *illa famosa loco quae appeletur Cyningestun in regionae Sudregiae* {18}. Local historians have made much of this description in the past, but it is doubtful whether it really signifies that Kingston was particularly well known, since similar phrases are commonly applied to other *villae regales* or 'Kingstons'. Probably the significance is that the place was known or designated locally as the centre for such royal administration as existed (for collecting renders, etc.). On post-Domesday evidence the area of the royal demesne administered from our Kingston was the two hundreds of Kingston and Elmbridge {19}. Apart from the late-Saxon royal inaugurations, there is little evidence to justify an inflated reading of the phrase *illa famosa loco,* Kingston is not identifiable as one of the *burhs* (forts) in the early tenth-century Burghal Hidage (and can therefore not be included among the Alfredian boroughs), nor is there any indication in Domesday Book that it was then regarded as a borough (unlike Southwark and Guildford). Formal incorporation only came with the 1481 charter, and though there is some earlier evidence of burghal features, it does not appear before the thirteenth century {20}. No coins have been found indicating that Kingston was the site of a Saxon mint, nor is there evidence of a bridge here much before the Pipe Roll reference to bridge repairs in 1193 {21}. We cannot as yet confirm, either, the existence of a bishop's hall before the Norman Conquest (there may have been a Saxon bishop's residence, but this is merely guesswork), or of a royal palace {22}. The Anglo-Saxon kings will probably have had a hall for their officials to hold courts, collect dues etc., but no very elaborate building need be visualised, for even centuries later the royal household was peripatetic, most of it living in tents (as, for example, with the Tudor court at Nonesuch). Finny's firm statement that Egbert had a palace in the Bittoms at the time of the 838 council is particularly misleading, for he had neither explicit documents nor related archaeological evidence. The Bittoms, probably marshy at this time, seems an unlikely site in any case {23}. The original parish of Kingston included not only Kingston itself but also Sheen (i.e. Richmond), the later Kew, Petersham, Ham, Hook, East Molesey and Thames Ditton, and the significance of this large unit with (eventually) its four dependent chapelries is that All Saints' Church was evidently established

4

as a minster, i.e. a missionary or teaching church for the whole area. But this should not be over-emphasised, for many royal estates were chosen as sites of minsters, including other Kingstons, and though some were established in the early Saxon centuries, others were comparatively late {24}. Archaeological evidence from the church site, slight though it is, hardly suggests an ancient foundation, nor are there any documentary pointers to early origin: the tradition reported by Leland (who did not believe it) that All Saints' Church had once been an abbey certainly cannot be cited in this connection, since it probably reflects a mistranslation of the Latin word *monasterium*, used for both minsters and abbeys {25}.

The precise site of late Saxon Kingston remains to be determined and any progress in this matter will now depend on what the archaeologists are able to discover. So far (though not from want of effort) few material remains from this period have come to light. In the 1976 excavation at No. 29/31 Thames Street, an interesting plot boundary was revealed, and this was dated from the ninth century to the tenth, which would be consistent with a site within a settlement founded by the Wessex kings after they took Surrey from Mercia in the early ninth century, shortly before the synod of 838 {26}. But clearly too much should not be read into a single discovery. If, as seems possible, the settlement was the normal nucleated 'vil', then this nucleus may have been defined by the 'four bridges of Kingston', as in the seventeenth century manorial documents, and these were probably Clattern Bridge, the Great Bridge, Barre Bridge (near where Wood Street turns right towards the railway station) and the Stone bridge (in Clarence Street, a little west of Marks and Spencers) {27}. The decision to develop the three-acre site between Bentalls and the Thames may help to clear up some of the prevailing uncertainty. The shorthand term for this area is 'the Horsefair', though the Horsefair proper was only the south-east quadrant (or less) of it. It was a mass of small properties before the Kingston Improvement Act of 1888, and this in itself may be significant, for the oldest part of a town often became slummy at a later date {28}.

1. [Both items are in **KBR** KX72/2/14. I have omitted several caveats referring to post-Conquest Kingston.]

2. [This blunt challenge to established perceptions of Kingston's past is characteristic of Miss Wakeford's fresh and independent approach to the town's history.]

3. For a general account of the crowning ceremonies, see **Sampson**, pp. 12-15.

4. M. Hinton in **SAC**, vol. 75,(1984), pp. 285-288.

5. W. E. St. L. Finny in **SAC**, vol. 38,(1930), p.229: and more recently, **SAS(Bull)** no. 174, (1981); no. 181, (1982).

6. J. E. Wakeford in **SAC**, vol. 75, (1984), pp. 251-256.

7. **Leland**, vol.. IV, p.85.

8. **Biden**, pp. 4, 5 & 6, note 'h'; and for more detailed discussion, J. E. Wakeford in **SAC**, vol. 75,(1984), p.255. [The exciting Roman discoveries in the Eden Street area (**SC** 7th. July 1989 p. 12) came after Miss Wakeford's death.]

9. See, e.g., P. Hunter Blair, *An Introduction to Anglo-Saxon England*, (1960), ch. 1; H. R. Loyn, *Anglo-Saxon England and the Norman Conquest*, (1962), ch. 1.

10. M. Gelling, *The Early Charters of the Thames Valley*, (1979), pp. 148-152 (nos. 308, 309, 311, 314, 315). Most are fabrications but may embody some authentic material or record a genuine transaction.

11. **PNSurrey**, pp. xi,xvii.

12. Bede, *Historia Ecclesiastica*, bk. iv, ch. 7.

13. **PNSurrey**, pp. 105-107.

14. *ibid.*, pp.1-2

15. **Britannia**, pp.13-14.

16. *ibid.*

17. *Oxford Dictionary of English Place-Names*, ed. E. Ekwall, (1960) - 'Kingston'.

18. P. H. Sawyer, *Anglo-Saxon Charters*, Royal Historical Society, (1968), pp. 403-404(no. 1438); and for the significance of the council, E. John, *Orbis Britanniae*, (1966), p. 37.

19. See, e.g., M. Cam, *Liberties amd Communities in Medieval England*, (1963), chs. 5 & 6. [For more recent discussion, see P.Sawyer, 'The royal tun in pre-Conquest England' in *Idea and Reality in Frankish and Anglo-Saxon Society*, ed. P.Wormald et. al., (1983), pp. 273-299.]

20. A. J. Robertson, *Anglo-Saxon Charters* (2nd. ed., 1956), pp. 246-249; D. Hill, 'The Burghal Hidage: the establishment of a text.', *Medieval Archaeology*, vol. 13, (1969), pp. 84-92.

21. [See below, Paper II.]

22. [For 'Bishops Hall', see below, Paper VI.]

23. W. E. St. L. Finny, *Clatrung, Clattering and Clattern Bridge*, Kingston upon Thames, (1938), p. 1. He is more circumspect in his earlier work, e.g. *The Royal Borough of Kingston upon Thames*, (1902), p. 40; *The Kings and Kingdom of Wessex*, (1931), p. 75.

24. The original parish was divided in 1769: **KBR** KA5/1. [For more recent work on pre-Conquest minsters, see J. Blair, 'Secular Minster Churches in Domesday Book' in *Domesday Book: A Re-assessment*, ed. P. Sawyer, (1985), pp. 104-142.]

25. **Sampson**, pp. 90-98; **Leland**, vol. IV, p. 85.

26. **SAS(Bull)**, no. 174, (1981); no. 181, (1982).

27. [See below, Paper III.]

28. [See also, J. E. Wakeford, 'The Horsefair Development', **KUTAS NL** 5, (March 1980): and for a broader picture, D. Serjeantson, 'The Kingston area in Roman and Anglo-Saxon times' in *The Archaeology of Kingston upon Thames*, ed. B. Woodriff, (1980).]

II

A NOTE ON THE SITE(S) OF KINGSTON BRIDGE

[Dating and locating the earliest bridge(s) over the Thames at Kingston are important matters both in their own right and in relation to the origins and early development of the town, but since little documentary evidence exists to illuminate these issues, answers will only come, if at all, through archaeological investigation. This brief note reviews the earliest written references in a way designed to assist local archaeologists. The main body of the paper forms the opening section of a draft dated 1972 found among Miss Wakeford's working notes (the remainder, dealing with the maintenance of the bridge in later times when it is known to have been on the Old Bridge Street line, is included below in Paper IX) {1}. The postscript is taken from a short note contributed to KUTAS NL 12 (May 1982).]

Although Biden confidently asserted that Claudius erected a wooden bridge over the Thames at Kingston, there is no reliable evidence for such a structure, or indeed for any bridge at or near the town before the Norman Conquest {2}. Edmund Ironside in his campaign against Cnut in 1016 crossed the Thames by the ford at Brentford, not at Kingston {3}. If, as Camden wrote in the sixteenth century, the ancient name was Moreford (meaning 'the marshy ford'), it would seem that the most prominent feature here when the English name was given was a ford, which had perhaps become too marshy when the general level of the river rose in post-Roman times {4}. A deed of 1323 refers to land 'against le More', which must have been near the river well upstream of modern Kingston, possibly somewhere in the Raven's Ait area, but the name is probably too general to have been used for only one site {5}. The name 'Kingston', however, is of an early type and is likely to have been given from the first to the administrative and fiscal centre of the royal estates here {6}. Assuming that the church is still on its original site (as seems likely from what Leland says about it), and was at the nucleus of the settlement, there seems no doubt that there had been a deliberate choice of a river-crossing site and almost certainly of one for a bridge, for here, as at London Bridge, there is for a very short distance solid ground on both sides of the river {7}. The problem for the archaeologists is to determine where, and, if possible, when this first bridge was built.

The area between the present bridge and the end of Vicarage Road seems now to be the only likely place for a bridge, but it is possible that the surface geology or the banks of the river have changed in historic times. In any case, the riverside for half a mile below this is now spoilt for archaeological purposes by Bentalls car park, the railway and the changes of levels made in the nineteenth century for the sewage works and later for the power station and Canbury Gardens. Even if we concentrate on the area between (say) the modern bridge and Water Lane, it is not possible to say where the earliest bridge may have been. It is clear from medieval title deeds that the present Old Bridge Street and Thames Street formed one street (called indifferently Thames Street or Thamesbridge Street) leading from the bridge round into the market {8}.

The earliest reference so far traced to this street is in 1360, by which time it already had buildings on its north side. We can say therefore that from at any rate the early fourteenth century to the early nineteenth the bridge was at the bottom of Old Bridge Street {9}. It is known however, that there was a Kingston Bridge in existence by 1193 {10}. This earlier bridge may also have been at the end of Old Bridge Street, but not necessarily, for Leland records among several interesting local traditions, that the bridge had formerly been lower on the river than it was in his time (i.e. below the Old-Bridge-Street line) {11}. Presumably the lower site had proved unsuitable either because it had been badly chosen (in which case it might be anywhere downstream) or, more likely, because extraordinary conditions, such as floods, had destroyed the bridge and possibly the settlement it had served. Camden lends some support to the idea of an early disaster when he writes of 'an older little town of the same name, lying low and subject to floods' {12}. There are no large scale maps of Kingston before the seventeenth century and the Gough map, now thought to date from the fourteenth century, shows Britain on too small a scale to include the bridge: it does not in fact show any river-crossing road in the Kingston area.

Postscript

In discussion at the Surrey Archaeological Society conference on Medieval Surrey in November 1981, Dr. D. Renn mentioned 1193 as the earliest date for Kingston bridge, and he later supplied the reference. Hitherto the earliest dates we knew had been 1219 and 1223 {13}. In the Pipe Roll for the year ending Michaelmas 1193 the sheriff of Surrey, accounting to the Exchequer for the 'farm' or annual rent of the county, deducts from it £2 13s. 6d. spent by him, by the king's order, on the repair of Kingston bridge when the king's army was there {14}. The army was presumably there because in 1193, while Richard I was abroad, his younger brother John's Welsh supporters were ravaging the neighbourhood of Kingston and Windsor {15}. and probably (as from time to time later) one side damaged the bridge to stop the other from crossing it {16}. As to the cost of the repair, Salzman gives the daily wage (without food) of a carpenter or mason in 1212 as 4d. {17}.

1. [KBR KX79/58;KX79/59.]
2. [For Biden's view, see above, Paper I, n. 8.]
3. ASC 'D' & 'E', sub anno 1016.
4. **Britannia**, pp. 13-14.
5. **PRO** E326/1607; E326/1610.
6. **PNSurrey**, p. 59.

7. **Leland**, vol. IV, p. 85.

8. [Old Bridge Street has now vanished beneath the Horsefair development.]

9. **KBR** KC16/1/26 (Tamesestrete).

10. [See below (postcript) for further details]

11. **Leland**, vol. IV, p. 85.

12. **Britannia**, pp. 13-14.

13. **VCH Surrey**, vol. III, pp. 488-489 and references.

14. ed. D. M. Stenton as *Pipe Roll Society* NS vol. 3, (1927).

15. *The Historical Works of Gervase of Canterbury,* ed. W. Stubbs, (Rolls Series 2, vols. for 1879, 1880), vol. I, p. 515.

16. **VCH Surrey**, vol. III , pp. 488-489: [also, below Paper IX].

17. L. F. Salzman, *Building in England before 1540,* (2nd. ed., 1967), p. 68.

III

WITHIN THE FOUR BRIDGES OF KINGSTON

[This paper was written for KUTAS NL 14 (February 1983) and can claim to be among Miss Wakeford's most novel and important contributions to modern perceptions of early Kingston's topographical development. The image of the medieval town as an island settlement, its boundaries defined on all sides by water and bridges, is ultimately rooted in an idea first put forward by local geologists {1}, but the way in which specific local features and detailed documentary references are woven together to give the idea a convincing historical dimension is entirely original. As printed here, the paper includes several detailed amendments appearing in a supplementary note contributed to KUTAS NL 15 (June 1983) {2}.]

If a 'catchy' phrase is one that catches on, 'within the four bridges of Kingston' must now be described as catchy. In a speech reported in the *Surrey Comet* last summer {3}, Kingston was even said to have been known as the town of the four bridges - thus are new myths born! Perhaps it is time to set out the rather tenuous documentary evidence for the use of the words.

So far I have found the phrase used only three times, and in only two documents, both in the Kingston Borough Records. In the Kingston court leet of 1st. June 1669, William Lidgould was accused of bringing in of furze bavins into his yard 'within the four bridges' contrary to an order {4}. Bavins were bundles of brushwood, a fire risk in a built-up area where hardly any building was yet in brick, so the offender incurred the heavy fine of 10s. {5}. I have not been able to discover where he lived or what his trade was. The substance of the order he had contravened was re-stated by the court of 9th. June (adjourned to 18th. July) 1674, which recorded that no person was to burn any furze or furze bavins 'within the four Bridges of this Town', under a penalty of 4s. each time {6}.

At the same meeting the court baron of Kingston manor considered the overgrazing of the commons. Orders of 17th. March 1633 on the subject mentioned at this court have not survived {7}, but new regulations were made. As to Norbiton Common (i.e. north of the Wanderings, now the road to New Malden), the 1674 orders provided that every inhabitant of the town of Kingston occupying any lands lying in Coombefield, Littlefield, Northfield or Berefield, whether the land be enclosed or not, might keep in Norbiton Common specified numbers of beasts proportionate to his acreage. Also every person 'inhabiting within the foure bridges in Kingston', or in Norbiton using or occupying any messuage, cottage or tenement held of the manor of Kingston which had been used for a dwellinghouse for the past 40 years, might keep in that common one cow, mare, gelding or nag {8}. The

10

VI. Pheasant Lane (now Vicarage Road) at the end of the nineteenth century. The decay and delapidation are typical of the riverside area of north Kingston at this date. (SC 20C 636).

V. Old Bridge Street c.1894 looking west towards the Thames. Ancient buildings of the kind shown here were common throughout Kingston until the present century. (**KHC** file print K1-230).

VII. This water colour by Hassell shows the southern entrance to Kingston Market Place as it crosses the Hogsmill bridge. The distinctive contours of the earlier bridge were drastically remodelled in Victorian times. (**BL** CRACH.1.Tab.1.B.1., vol IV, following p.330).

VIII. A view along the Hogsmill River as it passes through allotments on the outskirts of Kingston, 1928. A striking feature is the greater volume of water compared with today. (**KHC** file print K1-2833).

regulation of Surbiton Common was looser, because there was intercommoning by manors with adjacent common land, over which the beasts would stray. All tenants and occupiers of lands held of Kingston manor and inhabiting within the town of Kingston or hamlet of Surbiton might take benefit of the common at all times in a reasonable manner not surcharging the same. This is less precise than the Norbiton definition of a commoner but appears to equate living in the town with living within the four bridges.

The recent rapid acceptance of the phrase to define the town is due to its fitting so well the idea that Kingston was built on a gravel island between two channels of the Thames {9}. It also matches the documentary evidence, from the fourteenth century on, of a watercourse running north from the Eden Walk area towards Lower Ham Road, which seems to be the last remnant of the eastern arm of the Thames {10}. As to the origins of the phrase we know nothing, though presumably it became current at a time when there were four bridges in use, and possibly when the eastern arm of the Thames was still a major obstacle to movement. Certainly it is unlikely to have been invented for the seventeenth century manorial orders. The words trip out with the ease of long use, like saying 'up hill and down dale'. They seem to be a traditional way of saying 'in the town of Kingston', 'town' being where people lived, as distinct from the fields in which in earlier times most of them worked. Where, as in Kingston, the arable land was in several large open fields, worked in strips, the living-area would be the 'vil', the nucleus of the settlement (village or town). Tenants of house-plots there farmed the field-strips and had customary rights in the meadows, pastures, woods, etc. {11}.

[The four bridges are not specified in the seventeenth century documents, but can be identified without much difficulty from other sources. The Great Bridge over the Thames must be the first in any list, and Clattern Bridge over the Hogsmill stream just before it reaches the Thames is also an obvious choice. Less familiar and long since vanished are the Stone Bridge which took the road now called Clarence Street over the ancient watercourse on the eastern side of the town, a little to the west of Pratt's Passage; and Barre Bridge which must have crossed the same watercourse about where Lower Ham Road approaches Wood Street. The first of the quartet has been discussed on several occasions, and its status as a boundary mark is clear, for the Thames itself defines the town on the west {12}. However, the remaining three invite closer attention, especially in relation to the boundary issue.]

Clattern Bridge

The name occurs as early as 1293, but the structure is considerably older than this {13}. Confirmation of the significance of the Hogsmill as a boundary comes from a case in the King's Court in 1253, soon after the men of Kingston acquired the royal manor {14}. The dispute between Kingston and Merton Priory was partly concerned with the duties of the tenants of the Priory's manor of Kingston Canbury under the local peace-keeping system of keeping watch and following the hue and cry. The Canbury men said they did watch and join the hue and cry when and where they should, but also maintained that they had never been accustomed to watch beyond the water outside the vil of Kingston: within the vil they did as other men of the town

11

did *pro homine mortuo* (on account of a dead man), but not beyond the water which is at the end of the market towards Guildford. This limitation on their duties was probably claimed by the Merton tenants under Richard I's confirmation of Henry II's charter of 1165 to the Priory, which exempted them from most of the usual obligations 'excepting only justice of death and members' {15}. Their argument shows both that the vil was bounded (presumably on all sides) by water, and that there was water at the south end of the market, which fixes the Market Place on its present site as early as 1253. The northern limit of the market is not determined by this document.

The Stone Bridge

The bridge appears in, for example, two Kingston manorial quit-rentals of 1417 and *c*.1427, where some tenants live within and some without *Stonybrugge* {16}. A similar rental of 1383 uses instead the name *Bowebrugge*, which also appears in later records, an allusion no doubt to its profile {17}. In the seventeenth century it was Cross Keys Bridge, from the inn at its southern end, or sometimes it has the name of the owner of a site nearby, e.g. in 1679 Tanner's Bridge {18}. For centuries this bridge was regarded as a beginning and an end; King Street (later London Street), coming round the north-east corner of the Market Place, met Norbiton Street here. Watchmen's and rate-collectors' districts and the manors of Kingston and Canbury met here. Houses on the north side of the street near this point were referred to in Canbury manor records as 'in or near the town of Kingston' {19}, and even in the nineteenth century the Goldring family's gunsmith business premises and house, 39 Clarence Street (acquired by Bentalls in 1906) was said to be 'the last house in Kingston' - folk memories (and the conservatism of legal documents) from a time when buildings did not present a solid front along the north side of the street.

The main surviving Merton Priory record for Canbury Manor is part of a rental of about 1450, which includes a garden, formerly the vicarage, at *le Stonybrigge* on the south side of London Street near the Town Ditch {20}. The old vicarage, ceded to the Priory in 1376, had been described in 1352 as near a little rivulet and King Street, to the east of the church, situate between the said stream and the tenement and close of John de Kent {21}. The rivulet and the Town Ditch were evidently the same. By 1615 it is called a common sewer running from Heathen Street to Bowebridge {22}. In 1802, 3/4 of an acre of freehold garden ground was acquired by Peter Wood, a gardener, and on this occasion the land is said to be on the south-west side of a common sewer 'running . . . . towards and under a certain arch or bridge across the king's highway in a stret there called Norbiton Street' {23}. It was on Wood's bankruptcy in 1822 that his extensive gardens behind Clarence Street were sold, and one consequence of this was the creation of Pratt's passage {24}. A sketch map in a deed of 27th. May 1823 related to this process shows the water course {25}. About 71 ft. to the east of Pratt's Passage, the 'common sewer' emerges from a much wider sewer, which in Canbury Court rolls is referred to as 'the Great Common Sewer'. Alderman F. Gould, who had it filled-in in the mid-nineteenth century, remembered it as 8 ft. or 10 ft. deep {26}. It looks artificial (unlike the 'common sewer') and had probably been dug both for drainage of the silted eastern channel of the Thames, and as a boundary to Canbury manor, perhaps before it was given to Merton Priory about 1117. It was the back boundary of the Canbury properties facing the west side of Heathen Street (one of which was 190 ft. deep), and it is significant that the ground to the west of the great ditch (on part of which Young's Buildings stood in the nineteenth and twentieth centuries) was called 'Kingstons', as if to emphasise that when the drained land became usable, it belonged to Kingston and not to Canbury {27}.

The *Surrey Comet* of 20th. August 1864 provides an interesting postscript to the story of the bridge {28}. The paper had moved to an office in Clarence Street, just west of Pratt's passage, with a good view of the work then beginning on the Kingston system of drainage ('such as it was', as Merryweather said!) {29}. In the course of the excavations, the remains of the old bridge were brought to light. As the *Comet* noted,

'An old brick arch has given rise to a great deal of speculation and to rubbing up of the memories of the "oldest inhabitants" whose recollections do not entirely harmonise . . . . . we believe they are in the right who describe it as a ditch or cesspool, arched over, without any brick bottom to it. It extends only under the road, but is connected one way with an old open ditch that formerly ran along Clarence Street to the London Road, and on the north side with the ditch running through the Vicar's garden towards the outfall at the Thames by the side of the railway, at which point it was converted into a brick sewer when the railway was constructed. Underneath Clarence Street this ditch is much deeper than at the sides, there being a large hole or cesspool. The brick arch is at least five feet through. When first opened it was choked up with silt and other deposits, and a trial rod was pushed down for more than six feet without any bottom being found. After the top deposit had been taken off, water began to rise through freely and rapidly, showing that there was a clear passage beyond at all events. The crown of the new sewer will, we understand, be so low down as not to interfere with this old ditch' {30}.

Alderman Gould also remembered the old stream further north as an open sewer emerging from Clarence Street into the garden (on the west side of the former furniture shop on the corner of Fife Road) of Mr. Chapman, a barber, who used it to feed his strawberry plants! From this point the medieval stream was on its way to the last of the four bridges.

Barre Bridge

In 1355 when John Lovekyn gave the vicars of Kingston a messuage in the vil of Kingston for a vicarage-house, the site was described as next to the road which goes to the bridge *de la barre,* with the king's highway on the west and the town ditch on the east {31}. Nothing indicates that it was substantially different from the vicarage site of 1¹/2 acres bought (with its mulberry tree) by Bentalls in 1919, bounded on the west by Wood Street and on the east, according to nineteenth century maps, by a long rectangle of land about 80 - 100 ft. wide, running between Clarence Street and Lower Ham Road {32}. Presumably this was formerly a strip of waste representing the old stream bed and Town Ditch, later used for nursery gardens. In a survey of Canbury manor about 1679, the land on the east of this strip (also nursery ground in the nineteenth century) was called the Twenty Acres, formerly *Inholmes* {33}. Under the heading 'Purprestures' in a Kingston manor court roll of 1434, John Noreys was stated to have made an encroachment on the King's land at Barrebrugge, adding it to the Merton Priory land called the *Inhome* and thus 'disinheriting' or depriving the King (that is, the royal manor or Kingston) of it {34}. The measurements of the land taken in are stated to be 4 perches in length by 10 ft. in breadth. Noreys, presumably a tenant of the Priory, was fined 4d. for the purpresture. The name *Inhome* appears in Canbury records as *Inholme(s)*, indicating land taken in from waste, and thus suggesting a similarity to the Eden walk area {35}.

In 1356 John Lovekyn's endowment of St. Mary Magdalene Chapel in Kingston included 3 acres of land in *la Barrefeld* (later called Berefield) lying at *la Barre*, with a road called *Barreway* on the west {36}. Lower Ham Road was still called Bar(e) Lane in the seventeenth and eighteenth centuries. Medieval towns (and not only those with walls) commonly had at least one place called 'the Bar', where a principal road entered the town - witness, the Bars and Stoke above Bars in Guildford, Above Bars in Southampton, Temple Bar in London, the four bars of Banbury and North Bar in Beverley. In Kingston also there was 'a place anciently called by the name of the North Barrs' (no record has survived of a south or any other bar). The name may underlie the curious *Notebemes* and *Notebornes* in, for example, the rental of *c.*1427 referred to above, part of a south-north listing of streets etc. in Kingston running *Thamysebruggestrete, Northbythamyse, Notebornes,* and thus in the right area {37}. The Kingston Churchwardens' Account for 1503/4 shows that John Gervys paid 2d. 'for a garden at the North Bare corner . . . nov belded' (i.e. newly built, presumably a house or houses), and in the account for 1525/6 Tomasen Gervys (probably John's widow) paid the same for 'ii tenements at bare land ends' {38}. By the eighteenth century, houses at the place 'anciently called . . . the North Barrs' were changing hands and being rebuilt, and probably came into the hands of the Pembrook family, brewers, in the later eighteenth century {39}. From the bounds in the deeds it seems that the site was on the west side of Wood Street, between Vicarage Road and Water Lane (these are modern names), by the Two Brewers public house.

Several documents throw light on the stretch of the eastern arm of the Thames between Barre Bridge and the main course of the river. Reports from the *Surrey Comet* in the autumn of 1861, when the railway company was taking over part of the Downhall land by the Thames for the construction of the line from Hampton Wick to Kingston, note the company's argument that the land value was lowered by a 'public watercourse into which sewage had been put' which ran through the Vicar's garden {40}. This Downhall Ditch is mentioned in the many Town Council discussions on the new drainage system under consideration at the time, reminding us that Town Council minutes from the periods when the town was being greatly altered are a rich source of topographical information {41}. On one occasion, a committee considering the problem presented by the Kingston section of the Latchmere stream, recommended that it should be diverted to the Thames, in a barrel drain *via* Canbury Alley, into a large drain already existing in the Lower Ham Road -

14

evidently the Downhall Ditch {42}.

Although it is not yet quite clear what happened between some of the bridges, locating them gives a credible picture of the limits of the early town. If, as seems likely, Kingston was deliberately laid out on an island, there were no problems at the time in finding out who lived within the vil. The greater problem for us is why, if a dry island was available, the earlier Anglo-Saxon settlers chose to live further down the Thames on level ground much exposed to floods (as appears from reading together Leland's Itinerary and Camden's Britannia) {43}. We may suppose that it was a forced choice, dominated perhaps by existing roads leading to an old ford of the Thames, still much used even though, through changes in climate and river-level, it had become so wide as to merit the name Moreford (the marshy ford) which they are said to have given to Kingston's predecessor {44}.

1. [See below, n. 9.]

2. [See below, ns. 28,34 & 40.]

3. [Presumably the Summer of 1982, but I have been unable to trace the reference.]

4. **KBR** KF1/1/20.

5. [For early brick building elsewhere in Kingston, see below, Papers X ('The Three Coneys'), XI & XII.]

6. **KBR** KF1/1/25.

7. *ibid.*

8. *ibid.*

9. J. S. Penn & J. D. Rolls in *London & Middlesex Archaeological Society Transactions*, vol. 32.(1981), pp. 8-11.

10. See below, 'Barre Bridge' and n. 31.

11. Kingston had two field systems, each with several open fields. These were no doubt originally managed from two 'bartons' or granges called (because they lay north and south of each other) the north *beretun* and south *beretun* (later Norbiton and Surbiton): **PNSurrey**, p. 63.

12. [**VCH Surrey**, vol. III, p. 492: and above, Paper II.]

13. **PRO** E326/1102, *apud Clateringebrugende*. The earliest surviving features are dated late-twelfth century in **Pevsner**, p. 317.

14. **VCH Surrey**, vol. III, p. 492.

15. **Merton Records** , pp. 23, 44.

16. **KBR** KD4/1; 4/3.

17. **KBR** KD4/1.

18. **SRO** 58/1/1/8. For the name 'Cross Keys', see *Surrey Quarter Sessions Records: Order Books and Sessions Rolls 1666-68*, **SRS** vol. IX, (1951), p.192; also **KBR** KB1/1, p. 345.

19. **SRO** 58/1/2.

20. **SRO** 1179. I am grateful to Mrs. A. McCormack, Kingston Assistant Borough Archivist, who first identified this document and kindly gave me a copy of her transcription.

21. John de Kent held the Pratt's Passage land and may have been a tilemaker. The medieval vicarage is discussed in **Heales**, pp. 130, 163-167. [For Pratt's Passage, see below, Paper VI.]

22. **KBR** KC1/1/131.

23. **SRO** 250/6/66.

24. [See below, Paper VI.]

25. **SRO** 58/1/2/4, p.179.

26. **SC**, Diamond Jubilee number 1897.

27. **KBR** KC13/1/134; 13/1/135.

28. I am grateful to June Sampson for bringing this extract to my attention. [The paragraph from this point to the end of the **SC** quotation is taken from the supplementary note in **KUTAS NL** 15 (? June 1983).]

29. **Merryweather**, p. 30.

30. **SC** 20th. August 1864.

31. **Heales**, p. 225.

32. R. Bentall, *My Store of Memories*, (1974), p. 74.

33. **SRO** 58/1/1/8.

34. **KBR** KF1/1/1, f.1 (inaccurately transcribed in **Merton Records**, p. 298). [This section incorporates Miss Wakeford's corrections as set out in **KUTAS NL** 15(? June 1983).]

35. For the name 'Inholme' / 'Inhome' see **PNSurrey**, p. 272.

36. **PRO** SC11/629. (A transcript is available in **KHC**).

37. **KBR** KD4/3.

38. **KBR** KG2/2/1, pp. 35, 129. (A transcript is available in **KHC**).

39. **SRO** 42/34/1; 42/34/2: **SRO** 263/24.

40. I am grateful to June Sampson for bringing this report to my attention. [This paragraph is taken from the supplementary note in **KUTAS NL** 15 (? June 1983).]

41. **KBR** KB1/6 (to 1859), with subsequent volumes (1/7-1/25) running in unbroken sequence down to modern times.

42. **KBR** KB1/6, p.177: and for other interesting extracts, see M. Vaughan-Lewis's transcription in **KUTAS NL** 14 (February 1983).

43. **Leland**, vol. IV, p. 85: **Britannia**, pp. 13-14.

44. *ibid.*

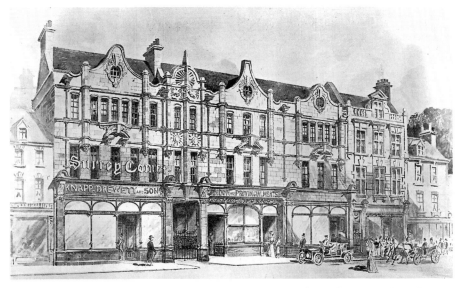

IX. The new Surrey Comet Offices in Clarence Street, 1900. It was from here that a keen observer noted the discovery of parts of the old Stone Bridge and common sewer during work on the town's drains. (**KHC** file print K1-2238).

X. An anonymous sketch of Acre Road in 1860. Much of the open land to the north was to disappear under housing in the next few decades. (**KHC** file print K1-276).

XII. The entrance gate to the Oil Mills in 1925, looking east from Oil Mill Lane, now Villiers Road. (**KHC** file print K1-3629).

XI. A wintery scene on the Hogsmill River c.1900, with the mill of the same name in the background. Again, it is the greater volume of water compared with today which impresses. (**KHC** file print K1-2866).

IV

THE LATCHMERE : AN ANCIENT BOUNDARY DITCH ?

[This paper is based on part of a supplementary note written as a corrective to Paper III above and included in KUTAS NL 15 (? June 1983). Since it deals with an issue distinct from 'the four bridges', it is printed here as a discrete item. Though a series of notes rather than a fully developed study, the paper demonstrates Miss Wakeford's ability to identify the historical significance of a seemingly unremarkable geographical feature, and as such shows how well she understood the nature of landscape history as it has been defined in modern academic circles. Of particular interest is the way in which late documentary sources are used to bring into focus developments of a much earlier time.]

The Town Council minutes of 6th. May 1852, dealing with the condition of the Latchmere river, contain several features indicating that this watercourse should be studied as a possible ancient boundary ditch, clearly artificial in places, even if originally made on the course of a natural stream (or several streams) {1}. In his history of the town, Biden regarded the Latchmere as a defensive boundary, but wrongly associated it with the name *Barre* (which had earlier been quoted as the name of a bridge) {2}. Without pretending to a real study, a few points are noted here in case others are minded to go into the matter.

The facts that almost the whole course of the Latchmere was on level ground (which I had not appreciated before reading the 1852 description) and that there was little movement in the stream, suggest that one of its original functions was to collect the water draining down over the clay subsoil from the Richmond Park area. One of the earliest references to it is *Lachemeres diche* in 1404, and this name occurs again in a deed of 1424, relating to land in the North Field of Kingston {3}. The Council committee in 1852 explained the considerable width and depth of the channel as the consequence of digging out the soil for manuring adjoining land, but presumably that would rather reinstate the original dimensions, the deposits being the fertiliser. These features all suggest a deliberately made ditch, but do not prove that it was dug, or even used, as a boundary.

According to the committee, the Latchmere rose in the Bullfields, an area lying between the Lovekyn Chapel land and Acre Lane {4}. The 1865 25-inch Ordnance Survey map shows traces of the east-west part of the watercourse in this area, by then not connected with the next section (shown also on the Kingston Tithe map of 1840) between the site of the Regal cinema/bingo hall on the corner of Canbury Park Road (where stood Mr. Row's house referred to in the 1852 minutes) and the Barracks in King's Road, previously Lord Liverpool's farm {5}. The only housing development shown in the vicinity of the Latchmere brook in Canbury ward at this time was that in the Cowlease area which followed the sale of the land in small plots in the early nineteenth century. There was little further building in Canbury ward until after the extension of the railway from Kingston to Norbiton and New Malden in 1869. The significantly named Cow Lease appears in a Canbury manor survey of 1679 as a close of 7 acres of meadow or pasture belonging to Nicholas Hardinge, who was both lord of the manor of Canbury and lay impropriator of the rectory of Kingston {6}. Cow Lease was bounded on the west by Canbury Lane (now Richmond Road), on the south by the common sewer (i.e. the Latchmere), and on the north by the Forty Acres (a close of arable land between the Cow Lease and King's Road, also held by Nicholas Hardinge). The survey also says of the Forty Acres that there was 'a footpath through the south side thereof leading from Kingston to London'. The Richmond Road end of this was presumably made into Acre Lane when the Cowleaze cottages were built. There is an interesting drawing of Acre Lane and the surrounding fields in the Kingston Heritage Centre collection of file prints {7}.

The course of the Latchmere between Cowleaze and King's Road is still traceable on modern maps as the back boundary between the houses in Acre Road and Elm Road. On the north side of King's Road it is the boundary between the Barracks and St. Agatha's R.C. Church. Just outside this church there is a stone with an inscription beginning 'The middle of the ditch is the . . . .' with the remainder not now legible {8}. From here, the watercourse ran north towards Park Gate House, outside the Ham Gate into Richmond Park: its course was (perhaps still is) marked by a line of alders running almost parallel to the north end of Park Road. Interestingly, a recent development near the Latchmere Road playground has been called 'Aldersbrook Drive'.

Further north, the watercourse was just within Richmond Park for some distance and then, with some evidently artificial sections, seems to be the 'south brook' of Sudbrook at Petersham. As early as 1211 Gilbert de Southbrook was one of three prominent residents of Petersham, which as part of the pre-Conquest endowment of Chertsey Abbey must have been defined in Saxon times {9}. From Sudbrook the watercourse on its way to the Thames at Petersham, according to 1852 minutes, entered into the High Road at Petersham. A barrel drain there is mentioned - the source of the trouble at the notorious 'Petersham Hole' a few years ago ?

The name Lachemere has been explained by one recent authority as 'pool by the sluggish stream', but this is not the only (as it is certainly not topographically the most likely) interpretation {10}. Lache is a Middle English word for 'a slow sluggish stream' (very apt here), but although the second element may be the Old English *'mere'* for 'pool', this is said to be 'very difficult, except on topographical grounds,' to distinguish from *maere*. The Old English *(ge)maere* meant 'boundary' and many examples occur of its use as a prefix to various elements which indicate an object to the boundary, though not, it seems, of its use as a suffix {11}. At least we may say that the conjunction of 'slow sluggish stream' with 'boundary' would be very suggestive for the Latchmere on topographical grounds.

1. **KBR** KB1/6, p. 177.

2. **Biden**, pp. 51, 108.

3. **PNSurrey**, p. 58 (under Ham). The 1424 reference is in **KBR** KC2/1/37.

4. For the Bullfields location, see **Ayliffe**, p. 15.

5. The Barracks site is now covered by modern housing, but the gate-house or 'Keep' (from which the estate is named) survives.

6. **SRO** 58/1/1/8.

7. **KHC** file prints, vol. 9, p.39:(K1-276). Beware vol. 3, p. 25:(K1-4132) which is the same drawing the wrong way round!

8. Information from Mr. B. Powell of Elm Rd., Kingston. [The stone is still in situ, but the inscription is largely hidden below pavement level.]

9. **Merton Records**, p. 66. Petersham is Chertsey Abbey land in Domesday Book: **DBSurrey** 8 (14).

10. **PNSurrey**, p. 58.

11. A. H. Smith, *English Place-Name Elements*, pt. II, **EPNS** vol.. 26, (1950), pp. 31-32.

V

SOME NOTES ON THE MILLS OF KINGSTON

[Apart from its role in determining the boundaries of early Kingston, water also contributed significantly to the town's economic life by providing fish (especially salmon), supporting osier and bullrush beds, offering good transport facilities for both people and goods and supplying power to local industries, especially milling {1}. The story of local milling remains to be written, but in sketching the topographical context in which it developed this paper makes a valuable initial contribution. Since the material survives only as a series of notes dated August 1978, evidently drafted to assist a private correspondent researching mill activity along the whole stretch of the Hoggsmill river, some editorial extensions have been necessary {2}.]

Domesday Book records five mills on the royal manor of Kingston, but since the entry describes an area that was greater than Kingston proper - e.g. it included Richmond - we cannot assume that they were all in the town, nor all on the Hoggsmill river {3}. [Some of Kingston's later mills may be the direct descendents of those recorded by the Domesday commissioners, but there is no conclusive documentary evidence for this, and if links are ever to be established, it will only be through archaeological excavation. What Domesday Book does show, however, is that the importance of milling in the economic life of medieval and early-modern Kingston was in all probability based on Anglo-Saxon precedents.]
    A local rating assessment of 1633 includes the following entry {4}:

The Mills
    John Chapman for Hogges Myll . . . . iiis.
    John Deacon for Middle Myll . . . . iiis.
    Robert Fyelder for Chapell Myll . . . . iiis.
    Richard Rose by goodes . . . . iis.
    John Riccards by goodes . . . . xviiid.

Richard Rose's was a windmill in Canbury, and the fifth mill was probably also a windmill, though its location remains to be established {5}. The other three were watermills, all on the Hoggsmill river and all originally cornmills. *Hoggsmill* (or *Hounslow Mill* as it was sometimes called) lay on or near the site occupied by the (now demolished) Coronation Baths at the junction of what are now Penrhyn Road and Denmark Road. It probably belonged to John Hog, who was active in local affairs around the turn of the twelfth century {6}. Later it was in the possession of Hounslow Priory, and in 1554 was sold by the Crown, to which it had passed along with other priory

20

XIII. Old Mill Lane (now Villiers Road) from the junction with Fairfield South, c.1902. The distant line of polled willows on the right marks the course of the Hogsmill River. (**KHC** file print K1-828).

XIV. The same stretch of Oil Mill Lane as in XIII, but from the opposite end, 1895. The line of polled willows, this time with luxuriant young growth, is visible on the left. (**KHC** file print K1-150).

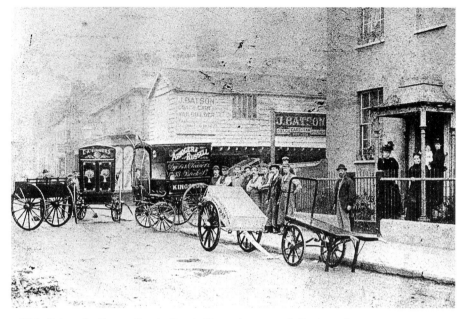

XV. Bateson's Forge, Brook Street (formerly part of Heathen Street) c.1900. The building lay on the eastern side of the street as it approached the Hogsmill River water-splash. (**KHC** file print K1-2947).

XVI. An internal view of the Tannery in Bishops Hall c.1930. The complex system of vats may have involved the adaption and reuse of older cellars. (**KHC** file print K1-3780).

property at the Dissolution {7}. In the early nineteenth century it was known as Mercer's Mill {8}. Subsequently it was used for the production of metal polish and was still remembered in recent times as 'Yewsabit Mill' {9}. *Middle Mill* at the bottom of Mill Street, leading off from Fairfield South, is mentioned in 1682 in the will of Richard Lant Esq {10}. It is here described, together with Chapel Mill as '4 watermills . . . .' held by Robert Boswell, so both were evidently 'double mills' {11}. In the nineteenth century, and probably earlier, it was used for the manufacture of articles from coconut fibre {12}. The Public House in Mill Street is still called 'the Coconut', no doubt to the puzzlement of many who now use it. There was an alehouse of the same name in Kingston in 1548, but not necessarily in the same place {13}. *Chapel Mill* or *Oil Mill* lay in Villiers Road near the modern entrance to the new industrial estate. Its earlier name derives from the fact that it formed part of Lovekyn's endowment of the Mary Magdalen Chapel in Kingston in the early fourteenth century {14}. At the Dissolution it passed with other Chantry lands to the Crown, but was soon sold. At the time of the sale it was described as two mills under one roof, so evidently was already functioning as the 'double mill' that is subsequently mentioned in Richard Lant's will {15}. In 1633, as noted, it belonged to Robert Feilder, who was the father of John Feilder, a pioneer local Quaker {16}. [A sequence of documents in the Borough records providing an unbroken descent of title to the mill from the late seventeenth century down to the nineteenth includes a detailed plan of the mill and its lands in 1835, and an abstract of title to the property in the mid-nineteenth century. Among material in Surrey Record Office is a second plan (of 1859) together with an interesting inventory of the milling machinery of a few years later {17}. By this time it was being used for the production of linseed oil, a fact reflected in its change of name {18}. Old Mill House, the residence of former mill owners, still survives a short distance from the site of the mill itself and is now the oldest extant building in this part of Kingston {19}].

Attention was drawn some years ago to an 'old mill' mentioned in documents of the sixteenth and seventeenth centuries relating to former Charterhouse properties in Kingston {20}. This seems to be distinct from any of the mills discussed so far, though the tentative identification of the building with the Guildhall site cannot be regarded as established. A much more likely location is somewhere in the Bittoms area. The mill is mentioned incidentally in Charterhouse documents concerning a garden and barn belonging to (but physically apart from) the George Inn in the Market Place which are described as lying in a back lane of Kingston 'by the old mill' {21}. The language implies that the mill itself was not Carthusian property, and this impression is strengthened by medieval and early-Tudor rentals and also by early property deeds relating to Charterhouse possessions in the town {22}. A search of these records has revealed only one reference to the mill, and again its presence is incidental. The reference occurs in a rental of 1446/47 which describes a quarter acre of Charterhouse land in *Tenterfield* as being bounded on one side by a mill formerly belonging to Robert Skerne {23}. Robert Skerne was paying quit-rent to Kingston Manor in 1417 for various properties in Surbiton, including a mill, and a will of 1486 refers to land near *Skernsmyll* in the context of a sequence of bequests involving land in the Surbiton area {24}. [There are several reasons for siting this mill in or near the Bittoms,

21

which though some distance from the modern town of Surbiton, was much closer to the original centre of the settlement and formed part of the medieval field system managed from the south *beretun* {25}. Much of the Bittoms area lay within the *Tenterfield,* and some of it, including the significantly named George Close, just west of the modern Penrhyn Road, was Charterhouse property {26}].

Also there is a mid-eighteenth-century reference to 'Backmill Close' on the site of Surrey County Hall, which seems more likely to have derived its name from a mill in the Bittoms area than from Hogg's Mill {27}. Finally, if Skerne's mill was a watermill not a windmill, there is a possible site for it on the Hoggsmill river as it passes across the top of the Bittoms. The site in question is marked by a big loop in the river due west of Hogg's Mill, seen in Hornor's 1813 map and also in the 1840 Tithe map, but later straightened out. This loop looks very like an old mill leat. In the eighteenth century, land on either side of this loop belonged to the Rowlls brewing family, held by them subject to a £3 annual rent payable to the town Grammar School. Some of this land had originally belonged to the Charterhouse, and subsequently was included in the original endowment of the Grammar School in Queen Elizabeth I's time {28}.

Another Kingston mill, known as Downhall Mill, lay in Water lane on the north side of the town {29}. No reference to this mill or to the name Water Lane has been found before the nineteenth century. It was evidently a steam mill, and there are interesting photographs of its interior in Kingston Heritage Centre {30}. [The only other mill in the Kingston area for which there is clear evidence is the windmill at Surbiton. Known to Ayliffe as Jenden's flour mill, it stood on the western side of the Ewell Road, between the modern Oakhill Crescent and South Bank {31}.]

1. [For local background, see **Sampson**, ch. III.]

2. [For Kingston's milling industry, see **Sampson**, pp. 49-50; also her more recent *All Change*, (1985), pp. 107-116, and J. Hillier, *Old Surrey Watermills*, (1951).]

3. **DBSurrey**, 1(8).

4. **KBR** KG5/2/1.

5. For Rose's mill, see **SRO** 212/64/19. In 1705 it is described as lying in Barefield: **KBR** KB1/1, p. 346.

6. **Merton Records**, pp. 39,41, 59.

7. **CPR** 1554-55. pp. 116-17.

8. **Ayliffe**, p. 46.

9. There are early photographs in **KHC** file prints.

10. **KBR** KB33/1.

11. For the 'double mill' arrangement, see *Medieval Archaeology*, vol. XI, (1967), p. 253.

12. **Biden**, p. 108: J. Sampson, *All Change*. (1985), pp. 110-111.

13. **KPR(M)** 3rd. June 1548, where bride and groom are described as 'servants of Mr. Wyllyams of the Cocoanut'. The Mill Street Coconut was 'The Joiners Arms' at the time of the Tithe Survey: **SRO** P33/2/1, plot 1464.

14. **CPR** Edward III, vol. 9, p. 363; vol.. 15, p. 15. See also, M. Vaughan- Lewis in **KUTAS NL** 10 (October 1981), where the earlier name of *Poleteres Mill* is recorded.

15. **Heales,** p. 198. [See also, n. 10 and n. 11 above.]

16. J. S. L. Pulford, *The First Kingston Quakers,* (1973), p. 28.

17. [**KBR** KP2/2/1-40 (the 1835 plan is with items KP2/2/33-34); **SRO** 2302 (the 1865 inventory is with item 2302/3).]

18. [The change is reflected in the former name for Villiers Rd., i.e. Oil Mill Lane. There are numerous photographs of the old lane in **KHC** file prints.]

19, [**Pevsner,** p. 318 suggests late-eighteenth century. For a more detailed architectural assessment, see J. W. Wakeford and I. J. West in **KUTAS NL** 24 (February 1986). This confirms a late-eighteenth century date, perhaps c. 1779.

20. P. Basing in **SAC,** vol. 65,(1968), pp. 142-143.

21. **KBR** KC3/2/1; 3/2/2; 3/2/3.

22. **PRO** SC11/631;11/632; SC13/15/36. See, too, many of the deeds relating to Charterhouse property in Kingston in **PRO** E326/.

23. **PRO** SC11/632.

24. **KBR** KD4/2. The will (of Thomas Walter of Kingston) is abstracted in *Surrey Wills: Archdeaconry Court, Spage Register,* **SRS** vol. V, (1921), pp. 37-38.

25. [The maps by Rocque (1745) and Hornor (1813) show old Surbiton as a cluster of dwellings in and around the junction of what are now Penrhyn Rd. and Surbiton Rd., and along Surbiton Rd. in the direction of the cross-roads near the Waggon and Horses Public House.]

26. [The George Close is mentioned in **KBR** KC3/2/60-68. Land in the Bittoms is associated with Tenterfield and Little Tenterfield in seventeenth century deeds, e.g. **KBR** KC1/1/246; 1/1/216. An acre of land in this area is called *Tenteracre* in the sixteenth century, e.g. **KBR** KC3/2/2; 3/2/3; 3/2/41; 3/2/42.]

27. **SRO** 262/1/17-20.

28. **SRO** P33/2/1, plots 1401, 1410, 1411, 1432. The £ 3 rent mentioned in 1609 (**KBR** KC3/2/133) can be traced in the Grammar School accounts, **KBR** KB21/4/2.

29. Also mentioned by Basing, above n. 20.

30. There are illustrations in **KHC** file prints.

31. [**Ayliffe**, pp. 43-44: K. G. Farries and M. J. Mason, *The Windmills of Surrey and Inner London,* (1966), p. 207.]

VI

OBSERVATIONS ON SOME LOCAL TOPOGRAPHICAL NAMES

[Over the last half-century or so, the interpretation of place-name evidence in its various forms has established itself as a standard technique of local landscape history {1}. Kingston, like other English towns both large and small, fostered a sizable crop of interesting names for its streets, alleyways and other localities, though few of those now in use are ancient, and most of the earliest names await rediscovery in local documents. The present paper reflects Miss Wakeford's long-standing interest in, and her thorough understanding of, the historical 'message' of place-name evidence. 'Heathen Street' was among her earliest writings, appearing in KUTAS CHRONICLE for May 1974. 'Bishops Hall' (undated) and 'La Royle' (February 1979) were found among her working notes, the latter having been drafted in connection with excavations on the site of the Guildhall Extension II. 'Pratt's Passage' was written for KUTAS NL 11 (March 1982). As variations on a single theme they combine to form a convenient whole {2}.]

Heathen Street

Heathen Street (now Eden Street) existed at least as early as 1315, when it was mentioned in a deed as *la Hethenstrate* {3}. It is one of about six Kingston street-names which first appear in the late thirteenth or early fourteenth centuries. Although the present Brook Street (which led to Hoggs Mill) was also later called Heathen Street, it was previously *(H)Oggestrete*. Documents from 1388 to *c.*1427 show the change {4}.

Heathen Street turned to the west as Eden Street does now and this curve is interesting. What did the street encircle? The documents do not tell us, for as far as one can see they relate only to properties on the margins, not to whatever was in the middle. If it was marsh and waste ground until perhaps the seventeenth century, that would not be inconsistent with the gardens and orchards of the eighteenth century and later. The street would be the more solid bank round the marsh and probably this geology also underlies the buildings on the west side of Eden Street as it approaches its junction with Clarence Street. Here in former times stood Hercombe Place, which retained the name of its late fifteenth century occupier and was said by John Aubrey in the 1670s to have been on land owned by Warwick the King-maker {5}.

The 1315 reference is to two shops in *la Hethenstrate* (apparently on the west side), which may well have been there before 1290, when the Jews were expelled from England. The idea that this was the Jewish quarter seems to come from Biden in the mid-nineteenth century. He says that the name of the street 'is probably derived from the circumstances that Jews, formerly excluded from towns, and considered Heathens, dwelt there' {6}. There is no evidence for the proposition and the two firm statements are incorrect. One can think of many medieval towns where the Jews, so far from being excluded, were at the centre: their area is usually called the Jewry or Jury Street (e.g. St. Lawrence Jewry near the City of London Guildhall), but never, as far as I know, Heathen Street. The Jews were not in fact regarded as heathens; the term is used for the followers of polytheistic religions.

The only comparable name I have been able to find is that of the place now called Haven Street, Isle of Wight. This was originally *la Hethenestret*, meaning 'street made by heathen men' {7}. This phrase recalls the language of the *Anglo-Saxon Chronicle* (e.g. A.D. 835 'In this year heathen men ravaged Sheppey'), where the 'heathen men' were the Danes. To explain our Heathen Street in the same way might please those who believe that Kingston's Shrove Tuesday football was originally the head of a Danish chieftain defeated here long ago, but I doubt if we should do so {8}. It was only in the time of Cnut (1016-35) that the Danes were here long enough to have made a road. The king undoubtedly used Kingston as his Saxon predecessors had done, for at least two of his charters were given here in the presence of a large assembly of notables {9}. But Cnut was an ostentatiously Christian king, so that it seems unlikely that the tenants of his Kingston estate would have been so tactless as to have called a road associated with the Danes *Hethenestret*.

Perhaps therefore we should look further back for our explanation, back to the origin of the word 'heathen' itself. Like 'pagan' (meaning countryman), 'heathen' once had rustic associations and both acquired their modern sense because the country people clung to their ancient gods while Christianity was developing in the towns. We do not know whether, or for how long, 'heathen' may have retained, perhaps in popular or local usage, the secondary meaning of an uncouth, superstitious rustic who lived out on the heath or waste, nor do we know when the street was named. But if we think of Kingston in early medieval times as a nucleus of dwellings near the church and river, we may believe that those who lived a hand-to-mouth existence outside it, on the banks of a large area of stagnant water or marsh, could have been called 'heathens' in this old sense by the more sophisticated (just as our grandfathers would have called them 'gypos'). There is some support for this in the old name for a lane running between Heathen Street and Littlefield, now represented by Fairfield Road. The name was variously spelt *Veldereslane*, *Felderelane* and *Felderislane*, and was presumably the place where 'felders' lived {10}. In Middle English this word meant rustics, those who worked in the fields or lived outside the town (as distinct from those who held tenements in the town or village and strips in the common fields). The felders would have been the same sort of people as the 'heathens' and when local industries developed, it would have been among them that the lowly and dirty jobs such as pot-making would have been found. The medieval kiln found some years ago was just behind Heathen Street and *Feldereslane*, and if the archaeologists are able to dig closer to the west side of Heathen Street also, they may find evidence of other trades, as they already have on the Union Street side of the area. The leather workers were apparently on the east side of the Market Place, perhaps where the Apple Market is now, but any trade which required great heat or caused much smoke or smell would be in just such an area as the early Heathen Street. John Hunte 'skynner' held land there in about 1427, but if he had a tanyard it was probably near the Hoggsmill brook {11}. There was a wheelwright's in Heathen Street in 1599, so Batson's Forge may have a long history {12}.

The trades practised in Heathen Street are not usually apparent from the fourteenth century deeds (which name landlords, not tenants) nor from the only surviving medieval rental of the Kingston properties of Merton Priory. This document dates from about 1450 and shows that at this time Merton Priory owned land on both sides of the street, as did the manor of Kingston Canbury in the seventeenth century {13}. Little is known of the early history of this manor, but possibly the closes of its tenants represent land already 'developed' (i.e. in the modern sense of 'built on') when the manor was given to the priory in the early twelfth century. In that case they may well have been inhabited before the Norman Conquest, and this seems quite likely in the case of our 'heathens'. An unwalled medieval town would develop suburbs with gardens and orchards and the noxious trades would disappear. The fifteenth century Merton rental gives indications of this, for it shows two 'tofts' (closes on which there had been but was no longer a building) and one of them (on the west side of the street) had once been held by Geoffrey *le Potter*. The other properties were houses with gardens, barns and in one case a *columbarium*, the large medieval dove-cote {14}. That part of Heathen Street immediately north of the former Three Compasses (now covered by Eden Walk) however, gives the impression of having always been small plots occupied by tradesmen, probably in earlier times making what they sold, and this is perhaps a further confirmation that the land behind the street-frontage became usable at a relatively late date.

As the car-parks and supermarkets go up, it becomes increasingly difficult to visualize this part of Kingston as it was even in the eighteenth century, when John Hall the Hogman kept his pigs in what is now Fairfield Road. The more desolate picture of 900 years ago or more demands an even greater effort of the imagination and 'finds' from the ground are likely to be more stimulating than references in documents {15}.

Bishops Hall

Bishops Hall takes its name from nearby property belonging to the Bishops of Winchester in the Middle Ages. This property lay on the north side of the lane and was bounded on the north by another property and on the east by several others, which fronted Thames Street and were probably of the same depth as now. The Bishop's 'Hall' may thus have faced towards the Thames, with steps and mooring at the water's edge {16}. The river was perhaps not so far west as now, for elsewhere (e.g. south of the old bridge and behind High Row, the west side of the Market Place) land was gained from the Thames by about 1500. In the seventeenth century, the Corporation had rent from 'a little tenement and wharf' at Bishops Hall, but the exact site has not yet been identified: contemporary records of repairs at 'Bishops Hall' thus refer to the locality, not to the medieval hall {17}. Apart from this doubt about the river frontage, the Bishop's land is clearly the same as the

26

nineteenth century property of the tanyard shown as plot no. 2145 on the 1840 Tithe Map, except a cottage property facing the lane, which had belonged to Canbury Manor and was bought by the tanyard owners in the eighteenth century {18}. There was a creek at Bishops Hall in the mid-sixteenth century with a watercourse running from Thames Street into the Thames, presumably down the lane {19}.

The Bishops of Winchester acquired land in Kingston in 1202, and their manor house at Esher was probably used from the mid-thirteenth century. Episcopal documents are dated from either Esher or Kingston (or of course from other Winchester houses) in that century, but increasingly from Esher towards its end {20}. However, the earliest known lease of the hall to a layman is as late as 1391 {21}. A tenant, Thomas Herland, is said to have entertained Henry V there in 1414, but as he was a beer-brewer, it may then have been an inn {22}. Thereafter it was used, as Leland said in the 1540s, as the ordinary residence of a townsman {23}. There is no indication of the structure of the Hall, except that in 1599, a Swiss traveller, Thomas Platter, wrote that he had looked over 'the stately residence of an archbishop (*sic*) in Kingston' and though he says nothing else about it, the words suggest that he saw the original building. It would then have been about 400 years old, so must have had sound foundations and could have been of stone {24}. The hall must have decayed or been demolished in the early seventeenth century, for by 1664 there was a tanyard there {25}. In the frugal way of our ancestors, they are very likely to have used the cellars of the hall as vats for the tanning. The installations are hatched on the 25-inch Ordnance Survey map of the 1860s and are on the east of the site, next to the boundary of the Thames Street properties. There are photographs of the interior of the tanyard in Kingston Heritage Centre {26}.

La Ryole

In the mid-nineteenth century, on or close to the site now occupied by the Guildhall Extension II, 'some beautiful early capitals and bases of piers' were found {27}. These were subsequently associated with King John's palace, said to have been located 'immediately to the south of Clattern Bridge, occupying the site of the road and line of houses', i.e. the buildings between the bridge and 17 High Street {28}. The only survivor of these finds is the pier outside Kingston Central Library, recently dated as *c*.1300 {29}. A photograph of 1899 in the Kingston Heritage Centre shows the pier standing on a plinth (as now) in a garden by a stream, presumably Mr. Coppinger's Creek House {30}. This is not necessarily where it was found and the garden is more likely to have once been part of the bed of the Hoggsmill. The house from which the stonework came seems to have been on land called *La Ryole*, a name already current in 1304 {31}. It was still in use 200 years later, for the Kingston Churchwardens' Accounts of 1503 record Master Bartellmere paying 10d. rent for lamps for property including a 'tenement later Tarrelton which. . . . . lyeth be ye common brok at ye ryall' {32}.

In the City of London there was a large house in Vintry Ward (the district of the wine importers) called *la Ryole* after La Reole, near Bordeaux, from which wine was imported {33}. Bordeaux wine became popular in England in

27

the thirteenth century (Gascony being an English 'colony', held as a fief of the French crown,) and was imported in large quantities, especially through London and Southampton {34}. The coincidence of the name in London and Kingston may indicate that a City wine merchant had a house in Kingston, which might well be the stone building of c.1300. Other great London merchants certainly had property in Kingston at this time, for example the Lovekyns, who were stockfishmongers but in Kingston were involved with some inns and taverns (i.e. wine shops) {35}. The name *La Ryole* might indicate a direct wine trade to Kingston, since wine had to go by water as far as possible. There could have been wharfs or a creek near the house (wharfs were not paved in Kingston even in the eighteenth century), although Clattern Bridge might obstruct boats coming up the stream.

Part of the Ryole area in Kingston was called the Ryall Farm, a name first heard of in the late fifteenth and early sixteenth centuries when it was owned by the Skern family, who also owned Downhall {36}. They probably built the large house called 'King John's Dairy', which was demolished in 1885 and seems from pictures to date from the late fifteenth century {37}. In the late nineteenth century it was described as having panelling and a fireplace in Elizabethan style, but other features of possibly c.1490 {38}. There was no question of its dating from King John's time (nor of course did the stone house from which the pier outside the Library came). Modern work on Plantagenet royal building makes it clear that there was no post-Conquest palace in the Kingston area: it is possible that a royal consort had property of her own here, but in any case kings on their travels stayed in any suitable house, priory, etc. {39}. The name 'King John's Dairy' certainly springs from the corruption of 'Ryall Farm' to 'Royal Farm', apparent from the Corporation's deeds relating to Cleave's Almshouses {40}. The Evelyn family, who invested heavily in property in Kingston in the later sixteenth century, had the Ryall Farm by 1585, leasing it at that date to William Stoughton, a butcher {41}. They sold the property in 1605 to Robert Tyffin, a brewer, who built brewhouses on part of the land {42}. After Robert's death as a bankrupt, his sons Thomas and John, also brewers, sold these brewhouses to Thomas Cleave, and they subsequently formed part of the endowment of the Cleave's Almshouses in 1668 {43}. The Ryall Farmhouse itself and the rest of the farm were bought from the Tyffins by Mr. Browne, 'Clark of the King's Spicer' (evidently concerned with the supply of provisions to the Court), and were later said to belong to Sir Anthony Browne, the owner of Downhall {44}. But Thomas Tyffin was apparently still living there in 1633, and another brewer, Mr. Yates, paid Hearth Tax there in 1664 and 1674 {45}. It may be that these brewers ran it as an inn (and that this had also been done in the sixteenth century), but there is no evidence for this and no inn-name has been traced: records are however scarce and formal at this time.

The immediate neighbourhood (both sides of West by Thames Street and the first part of Bittoms Lane, once the main road to Surbiton Street) seems to be the area of the early breweries, i.e. from the second half of the fifteenth century when the use of hops made the brewing industry possible. Thereafter brewing and inns were a good investment for the gentry and professional classes, such as the Evelyns. There is no indication that the Skerns were brewers, or that they lived at the Ryall Farmhouse. It was used as a residence

XVIII. An undated photograph of the building popularly (but erroneously) called King John's Dairy. It stood on the eastern side of High Street, a little distance beyond Kingston Police Station. (**KHC** file print K1-1178).

XVII. Photographed here in 1899 in a private garden, this thirteenth-century pillar now stands outside the Public Library. It is said to come from a substantial stone building in the Bittoms area. (**KHC** file print K1-487).

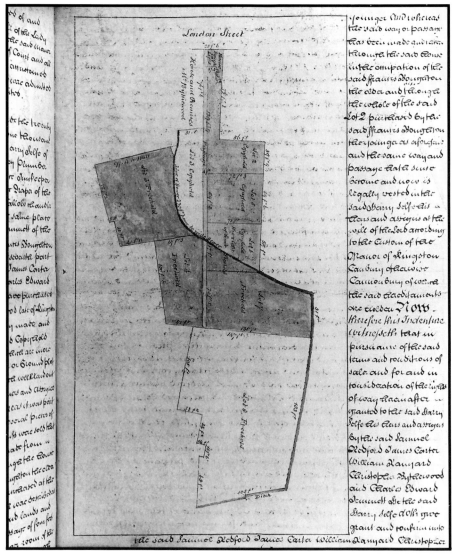

XIX. An early-nineteenth-century plan made at the time of the creation of Pratts Passage. It is especially valuable as a record of the course of the medieval town ditch, here described blandly as a sewer. (**SRO** 58/1/2/4, p. 197).

in the eighteenth century, and there was also a tanyard there. In 1784 the Rowlls family bought the Ryall farmhouse. In the Tithe Map of 1840, the original farmhouse site is represented as plots nos. 1360 and 1359, though the latter (the site of no 17 High Street, the former Steak House) was not now in the hands of the Rowlls family. They did, however, hold the nearby plots 1410 and 1411, which may indicate that these too had once formed part of this farm {46}.

Pratt's Passage

Pratt's Passage, the remnants of which have survived recent redevelopments on the western side of Marks and Spencers, is not quite the ancient right of way it might seem. The original passage, four feet wide, was made only in 1823, and was not a public right of way (it is now known as 'Right of Way no. 21'). The land through which it was cut was copyhold of the manor of Kingston Canbury and once the tenancies have been linked with their sites, information about it can be found in the manorial records in the Surrey Record Office {47}.

In the 1820s there were buildings (none of which has survived) on the street front from Marks and Spencer's round to the present Surrey Comet shop in Church Street. This was then called London Street, a name which was also often used for the stretch of Clarence Street (earlier Norbiton Street) from Marks and Spencer's to Eden Street. What is now more difficult to visualise is that in 1822 the land between Marks and Spencer's and Church Street was mostly nursery and market gardens. According to a deed of 11th. June 1822, most of it was owned by Peter Wood, a gardener and seedsman dealer, 'getting his living by buying and selling seeds, fruit, vegetables, etc.' who went bankrupt for a debt of about £ 100 to a gardener of Marlow, Bucks. {48}. His land was sold in 1822 in lots, of which Lot 8 was the Eden Walk area where the 13 cottages, still remembered as Young's Buildings, appeared soon afterwards. The purchasers of Lots 2-8 (i.e. of land in the vicinity of the passage) made it a condition of sale that a passage be made through the west side of the lower room of a house facing London Street, already belonging to Mr. Francis Boughton the elder, and through the west side of his yard, and should be continued southwards to the boundary wall of Lot 8. They joined in a deed of covenant dated 27th. May 1823 (enrolled at the Canbury Court Baron of 27th. October 1823), setting out their various interests in the land dedicated to the passage, each covenanting to maintain the section bought by him and to give the others a right of way {49}. So James Carter of Kingston, draper, the purchaser of Lot 8 (and thus the tenants of Young's Buildings) had access from Clarence Street: but as late as 1900 half of the width of part of the passage was treated in the Canbury manorial records as belonging to the owner of the adjoining copyhold land {50}.

Ayliffe says that Mr. Pratt kept a shop for leather goods, boxes and trunks next to (i.e. to the east of) the archway leading to Young's Buildings {51}. Since he does not appear in lists of local occupants for 1828, 1838 and 1839/40, Mr. Pratt probably opened his shop after 1840, and thus earned his place in Kingston's history {52}. He may have been related to that Peter Pratt who died in 1806 and who had been active in the revival of the

Congregational Church {53}. This man has been identified with the Peter Pratt who was a Thames Ditton churchwarden and who in 1784 figured in an extraordinary body-snatching episode involving Thames Ditton and East Molesey churches {54}. According to Ayliffe, Young's Buildings were known in the 1830s as Cato Street, 'from the fact that the original builder was connected with the famous Cato-street conspiracy'. The unrest in the country at the time of Peterloo and the Six Acts came to a head early in 1820, there was a plot to kill the whole Cabinet at a house in Grosvenor Square, where they were to dine, and the conspirators met in Cato Street, near the Edgware Road, but their plans were discovered in time {55}. An earlier enquiry into the matter failed to establish a definite Kingston connection, although a possible link may be provided by the presence of J. Shaw Strange among the conspirators: the name Strange occurs in Kingston in the early nineteenth century, though does not include builders {56}.

A concluding fact about Pratt's Passage illustrates how the conservatism of legal documents can preserve, or fossilize, the history of a property. The passage was cut through a property called the Gatehouse, which had a stable, yard and Apple Garden belonging to a house called the Cross Keys. In the mixture of Latin, French and English used in some legal documents for centuries, the property was said to include *unam Romeam vocat 'le drinkehouse'* and another room called *le Buttery* {57}. These phrases, in an even more garbled form, continued to be used as late as 1808, although by that time the buildings described had certainly disappeared {58}.

1. [For work in an urban setting, see E.Ekwall, *Street Names of the City of London*, (1954 etc.); *The Atlas of Historical Towns*, ed. M. D. Lobel, 2 vols., (1969,1975): *Winchester in the Early Middle Ages*, ed. M. Biddle, (1976).]

2. [For another example of Miss Wakeford's use of place-name evidence, see above, Paper I and n. 6.]

3. **KBR** KC16/1/38.

4. **KBR** KC16/1/44-5; KD4/3.

5. [For Hercombe Place, see below Paper VII.]

6. **Biden**, p. 8. [**PN Surrey**, p. 59 is more cautious. For Jewish influence in thirteenth century Kingston, see E. H. Bilefield in **KUTAS CHRONICLE** (August, 1972).]

7. ['Haven Street' (and some other examples unnoticed by Miss Wakeford) are considered in A. H. Smith, *English Place-Name Elements*, pt. I, **EPNS** vol. XXV, (1965), p.220. Canterbury had a *Heathenmenslane c.* 1220: W. Urry, *Canterbury under the Angevin Kings*, (1967), p. 171.]

8. **ASC** 'E', sub anno 835. For Shrove Tuesday football in Kingston see **Sampson**, p. 81 and illustration (of 1840) opposite p. 50. [The event is also discussed over a wider area in M. Alexander's paper in **SAC** vol. 77, (1986), pp. 197 ff.]

9. *English Historical Documents*, vol. I, c. 500-1042, ed. D. Whitelock (2nd. ed. 1979), pp. 596-97 (no. 130).

10. **KBR** K16/1/85; 16/1/94; 16/1/95.

11. **KBR** KD4/3.

12. For Bateson's Forge in Brook Street (formerly part of Heathen Street) see **KUTAS** Occasional Paper 1, (1974), pp. 21-23 and **KHC** file prints, vol. 8, p.14, (K1-2947).

13. **SRO** 1179 [(and above, Paper III, n. 20 for acknowledgement).]

14. For late-medieval deeds relating to this area, see **KBR** KC16/1/38-51.

15. [The substitution of 'Eden' for 'Heathen' is usually attributed to nineteenth-century religious scruples, but a mid-eighteenth-century reference to the thoroughfare as Christian Street suggests earlier anxieties: **Merryweather**, p. 15; **SRO** QS Bundles, Xmas 1769, nos. 18 and 23. A seventeenth-century attempt to render Heathen Street in Latin produced the valiant but bizarre *Ethnica Placea*: **SRO** 58/1/1/2, m. xvii. d.]

16. [The name is overlooked in **PNSurrey**. It occurs in the early fifteenth century as *Bysshopeshall* and in 1481/82 as *Le Bisshoppeshowe:* **KBR** KD4/3; KC1/1/69; **BL** Add. chr. 23529. For the river frontage issue see **VCH Surrey**, vol. III, p.490.]

17. See, e.g., **KBR** KD5/1/2, pp. 109, 116, 127, 129, 137.

18. For early-seventeenth-century references to the Canbury property here, see **SRO** 58/1/1/1. It appears regularly in subsequent Canbury manorial documents and was enfranchised in 1861: **SRO** 58/1/2/7, p. 9 (no 113).

19. **KBR** KC1/1/73.

20. **VCH Surrey**, vol. III, p. 490 and references.

21. **M&B**, vol. I, p. 345 (a lease by Bishop Wainfleet to Hugh Herland, his wife Joan and their four sons).

22. Thomas was the eldest of the four Herland sons: above, n. 21.

23. **Leland**, vol. IV, p. 85.

24. [I have been unable to trace this reference.]

25. **PRO** E179/188/481: **KBR** KC1/1/86.

26. **KHC** file of prints, vol. 11, pp. 22-23, (K1-1711; K1-1713).

27. H. P. Measor, *The Antiquities of Kingston* (lecture given 19th. February 1861 and published by Knapp later the same year).

28. ibid. **Biden** (published 1852) makes no mention of a royal palace in this area, so the idea presumably originated with Measor's lecture. It was taken up by, inter alia, Finny (above, Paper I, n. 23). The notion of a royal palace somewhere in Kingston is older. **Biden**, for example, notes that local residents sometimes located it on the site of the Castle Inn on the west side of the Market Place, but his own preference was for the so-called Warwick Castle site in Eden Street: **Biden**, p. 21, note 'o'; pp. 23-24, note 'p'. [See also below, Paper VII.]

29. **Pevsner**, p. 314.

30. **KHC** file prints, vol. 3, p. 5 (K1-487).

31. **PRO** E326/1695: and for other early references, **PNSurrey**, pp. 60-61.

32. **KBR** KG2/2/1, p. 34.

33. **PNSurrey**, pp. 60-61.

34. [For historical background, see M. W. Labarge, *Gascony, England's First Colony: 1204-1453*, (1976).]

35. **Sampson**, pp.78,102: **Heales**, pp. 147-248.

36. **CIPM**, vol. III, p. 1138: **SAC**, vol. 8 (1883), pp. 52, 118. The name 'Ryall Farm' occurs in 1599: *Surrey Wills: Archdeaconry Court, Herringham Register*, pt. 1, **SRS** vol. 3 (1915), pp. 106-107 (no. 471).

37. There are several illustrations in **KHC** file prints.

38. *Kingston & Surbiton News,* 16th. May 1885 (quoting a former Clerk of Works at Hampton Court).

39. No royal buildings at Kingston are noted in H. M. Colvin, *History of the King's Works,* vols. I & II (1963).

40. **KBR** KC3/1/1; KC3/3/17-21. 'Ryall' and 'Royal' are both freely used in Kingston manor court baron and quit-rent rolls of the seventeenth and eighteenth centuries.

41. **KBR** KC4/1/1; KC39/1.

42. **KBR** KC4/1/1.

43. **KBR** KC3/4/17.

44. **KBR** KC4/4/19.

45. **KBR** KG5/2/1: **PRO** E179/199/481; E179/199/496.

46. **SRO** P33/2/1. (plots 1410, 1411).

47. **SRO** 58/1/1-3.

48. **SRO** 58/1/2/4. pp. 173-178.

49. *ibid.*

50. **SRO** 58/1/2/6.

51. **Ayliffe,** p.19.

52. **KBR** KD8/4/1; KD7/1/8: **SRO** 474.

53. A. C. Sturney, *The story of Kingston Congregational Church,* (1955), pp. 23, 26, 27.

54. T. S. Mercer, *More Thames Ditton Tales and Scandals,* (1970), pp. 3-6.

55. **Ayliffe,** p.19. [For general background, see L.Woodward, *The Age of Reform 1815-1870,* 2nd ed., (1962), p. 66.]

56. The conspirators are named in **KUTAS CHRONICLE** for August 1973.

57. **SRO** 58/1/2/1.

58. **SRO** 58/1/2/4, p. 51.

VII

CRIME AND PUNISHMENT IN KINGSTON: TWO TOPOGRAPHICAL PROBLEMS

[Before the establishment of a police force in the nineteenth century, responsibility for maintaining law and order was principally borne by local communities. Towns in particular, because of their traditional administrative importance, more substantial resources and also perhaps because the problems there were proportionally greater, often spawned a varied range of public 'facilities' for coping with those whose behaviour was deemed socially and legally unacceptable. In the case of Kingston, some of these (the town or Stockhouse gaol in Clarence Street, the County Gaol or Bridewell in Eden Street) have been studied and their sites established {1}: but others, including the two discussed here, have gone largely unnoticed. 'The Gallows' was written in response to an enquiry sent to the editor of the KUTAS Newsletter and first appeared in NL 16 (November 1985): 'The Folly, formerly the Prison House' is an editorial contribution based on draft notes left by Miss Wakeford and augmented by information from sources known to her but which she was unable to examine. In both, the principal concern is with the issue of location.]

The Gallows

My enquiries into the location of the town Gallows were prompted by the following letter, sent to the editor of the KUTAS newsletter {2}:

'Some time last year on a general wander round Kingston, I found myself at dusk near the George and Dragon at Kingston Hill, so I went off in search of the Gallows Tree or some romantic curiosity which would enrich my imagination. I asked somebody who was going home after a day's exercise on Coombe Golf Course who directed me to a private section of about 200 yards in on the left side of George Road. I found, as he had directed, a mound and an appropriately ugly tree. Quite convinced that I was in the presence of historic importance, I took a well earned photograph and retreated. Whether it was authentic or not, hunting highwaymen at dusk did wonders for my imagination! How close did I get?'

We have usually assumed that one of the places where the gallows for the hundred of Kingston may have been over the centuries was somewhere near the spot north of George Road and now on the golf course, marked 'Gallows

Hill' on large-scale Ordnance Survey maps, and near the Gallows Conduit on the other side of that road. It is disconcerting to find no evidence that the gallows was there and no reference, earlier than the maps of the 1860s, for the name Gallows Hill there. As late as 1852 Biden knew Gallows Hill only as the place near Richmond Park wall {3}. The name Gallows Conduit is equally elusive. Its site is referred to in 1617 as a close 'whereupon the conduyt standeth' {4}. The earliest use of the name Gallows Conduit which I have so far found is on an undated, but presumably eighteenth century, plan of the conduits etc., of the Hampton Court water supply {5}. From this plan it looks likely that the conduit has been named because the gallows shown on the far side of the road over Kingston Hill was conspicuous from it. Gallows Hill is not marked.

The earliest map with the gallows marked seems to be that made for Charles I to show the land to be taken in for his New Park in 1637. The symbol for a gallows is on Kingston Common, between the park wall and the road over the hill. Within the proposed park there is a Gallows Slade nearby, but there are also Gibbet Wood and Close (on the other side of the hill but still in Kingston Hundred), between the present Isabella Plantation and the car park {6}. Rocque's 1746 map of ten miles round London has the gallows symbol and 'Gallows Hill' in the same area, and his smaller scale 1762 map of Surrey also places Gallows Hill there. The symbol comes between the site of the Fox and Coney and the point where the park wall has a sharp turn towards Kingston Gate. A description of the bounds of Kingston manor made in 1809 for the enclosure of common lands refers to a bound mark in the park wall upon Gallows Hill {7}. Presumably by this time the gallows had gone, since Ayliffe and later nineteenth century historians do not record any memory of it. After the enclosure, the site was occupied (according to the 1865 Ordnance Survey Maps) by a property called The Knowle, a name which seems to be a compromise between the Scots knowe and the southern knoll (both meaning a small hill or mound) and which may refer to a mound on which the gibbet had stood. The site is now on the Kingsnympton Estate.

It is not clear from the Ordnance Survey cards why Gallows Hill is shown as north of George Road, when Rocque has marked a quite different site. There is a much quoted passage from Leland's *Itinerary* about the remains of walls of houses discovered on the slope down from Coombe Park towards the gallows, and finds of Roman coins, etc. in Cardinal Wolsey's time (usually taken as indicating that they were made around 1520 during the construction of the Hampton Court water supply system - all of which seems to be between the modern George and Coombe Roads {8}. These reports may well be the only reason for placing the gallows of Leland's time and earlier in the George Road area - on the argument that it might be thought unlikely that the slope where the walls had been seen would have been described by reference to a gallows on the far side of the main road. Perhaps the Ordnance Survey simply followed the name Gallows Conduit, in ignorance of the site near the Park Wall. Once 'Gallows Hill' was in print on the George Road site, the 'tradition' of a gallows there would soon be established. The small triangle between the two words has probably been misunderstood as the actual site (it is the symbol for an Ordnance Survey triangulation station). Local papers mentioned the commemorative tree when the golf club house was moved to the other side of George Road.

There was another gallows on Surbiton Hill, the symbol for which appears on the east side of Ewell Road on Rocque's 1762 map of Surrey. Merryweather says that 'weird traditions of the gallows which it was said formerly stood on the hill distressed the minds of old inhabitants, and it was regarded as a somewhat dreary drive to venture after nightfall from Tolworth to the turnpike gate' {9}. But the Ewell Road of our day is no more evocative of the ghosts of hanged felons than is the Kingsnympton Estate.

The Folly, formerly the Prison House

A prominent feature of Kingston's sky-line in the seventeenth and eighteenth centuries, and probably in earlier times too, was a curious tower-like structure known as 'The Folly' or 'The Folly House', formerly 'The Prison House' {10}. It is illustrated in an anonymous pen and ink sketch dated 1770, known today only from a photograph in the Kingston Heritage Centre, and also in an undated coloured picture, again anonymous bound into R. Percival's grangerized version of Manning and Bray's County History {11}. Both illustrations have short explanatory inscriptions. In the note attached to the first, the tower is described as 'The Folly in a back street of Kingston upon Thames, called the Prison House', and we are also told that it 'belonged to, and was pulled down by Mr. Portman of The Sun some five years since' {12}. In the second note, the structure is termed 'an ancient brick building near the Bridewell of Kingston on Thames, Surrey, called the Folley (*sic*) pulled down in (blank) and (blank) Luxmore's house built on the spot' {13}. In addition to the pictures, there is this short written description of the tower by W.D. Biden:

> 'Within the memory of an aged person now living, a portion of a tower of five stories (*sic*), not unreasonably supposed to have formed a prominent part of the Warwick Castle, was still standing and used as a dwelling house. The stories had no internal communication but were approached by a flight of steps outside. A pillar remaining entire in the middle of the building was probably the axis of a spiral staircase. The tower stood nearly opposite Bridewell Alley' {14}.

Though not identified either as the Folly or the Prison house, it is clear from the physical details and from the reference to Bridewell Alley that Biden's tower and the tower in the two illustrations are one and the same.

The tower prompts obvious questions. When was it built, and by whom? Where did it stand? When precisely was it demolished, and what replaced it? Are its popular names accurate pointers to changes in function over time? If once used as a place of custody, how far must we now revise the established view that Kingston's ancient prison was the Stockhouse gaol, formerly standing in what is now Clarence Street? {15}. How convincing is Biden's suggestion that the tower began life as part of a castle built by Richard Nevill, Earl of Warwick, in the later fifteenth century? The existence of this castle is an established part of the popular folklore of the town, and has even drawn a measure of official recognition, but very little has been done to show that the building has a foundation in historical reality {l6}. Can the tower provide a means of correcting this deficiency? The principal concern of this paper is with the single issue of location, but hopefully others may be stimulated by the discussion to take up some of the additional questions to which the tower gives rise. At the very least, the following notes should bring to the attention of a wider audience the existence of an intriguing, and possibly important feature of Kingston's earlier topography.

The inscriptions accompanying the two illustrations and Biden's written description provide several clues to the approximate location of the tower. The reference to the Bridewell or old County Gaol indicate a site in or near Eden Street. Hornor's 1813 map of Kingston places the prison on the eastern side of the street, near its junction with Brook Street, close to the site now occupied by the town's Post Office, and the general accuracy of this placement has been confirmed by recent work. {17}. The alley to which the building gave its name ran further north, branching off at right angles to the street, following approximately the line now taken by Fairfield Road {18}. From the reference to Luxmore and Portman however, and also from Biden's phrase 'nearly opposite Bridewell Alley', it is evident that the tower lay on the western not the eastern side of Eden Street. Charles Luxmore paid rates and taxes for a substantial house in Eden Street from 1798 onwards, and a plan of 1823 enrolled in the court records of Kingston Canbury manor locates this property in very general terms south-west of the junction of the highway with Clarence Street {19}. On this basis, we can identify the house as the large mansion set in parkland that is the sole building of any real size in this area on Hornor's map {20}. Known later as 'Gough House', and occupying the site now taken by no. 57 Eden Street, the building survived well into the present century, finally surrendering to property developers only in the summer of 1929 {21}. Its construction was not Luxmore's work, but evidently occurred in the early 1790s on the initiative either of Jacob Hemmett or of William Tothill, or possibly both, the one commencing, the other completing the project {22}.

The decision to build on the site involved the destruction of an existing structure of considerable antiquity. Described at the time of its demolition as a 'mansion house or capital messuage or dwelling house', and known in the seventeenth century (and no doubt earlier) as 'Hercombe Place', this older building was presumably owned, and perhaps originally erected by John Hercombe, a prominent tenant and retainer of the Earls of Salisbury in the later fifteenth century {23}. His successors there were also in some cases men of more than local importance, including in the seventeenth century Richard Le Wright, at one time steward to the ill-fated Robert Earl of Essex, and later Keeper of the King's Jewel House {24}, and Robert Le Wright his son, a Bencher of Middle Temple {25}; and in the early eighteenth, George Cole, a wealthy merchant and Citizen of London {26}. Jacob Hemmett, owner of Hercombe Place in its final years, acquired the house in the early 1770s, but probably did not inhabit it for very long, since local rate books for the 1780s, though showing him still in possession, describe the building as 'empty'. The description suggests perhaps that the house was already substantially decayed when the decision to demolish it was taken {27}. Documents relating to the process of demolition and reconstruction say nothing of the Folly, mentioning only Hercombe Place as the antecedent of the new house, so the inscription on the Percival illustration, in a literal sense at least, appears to be mistaken.

36

As a general pointer to the approximate site of the tower, however, it may have more value, for the owners of Hercombe Place in the eighteenth century owed quit rents to Kingston manor not only for the mansion itself, but also for a string of other properties, one of which is described as 'a tenement next the Folley' {28}. The distance between the tenement and Hercombe Place is not immediately apparent, but was probably not very great, for the tenement heads a list whose order has clearly been determined on the basis of the relative proximity of the individual entries to the main house. Thus, the next entry in the list is 'a tenement late More's', whose site can be accurately located on the western side of Eden Street just to the south of Hercombe Place {29}; then come 'several tenements in Wheelbarrow Court' which we know formed part of the site subsequently occupied by Bridewell prison {30}, then a series of properties lying much further from the mansion in other streets or in the open fields around the town {31}.

A further clue to the location of the Folly House is the reference to Mr. Portman of The Sun. Two men with this surname occur in local documents of the eighteenth century, a father and son, both called Richard, both proprietors of The Sun Inn in Kingston Market Place, and both tenants of the Folly site {32}: but since Richard Portman senior died in 1769 within a year or so of acquiring his title, it must be the younger Richard who was responsible for demolishing the building {33}. His connection with the tower is established by a Kingston Canbury manor court entry of 28th. May 1791, in which he is described as having 'lately bought' three houses in Eden Street, one called 'The Folly House, formerly the Prison House' {34}. The entry omits the vendor's name, the exact date of the transaction and the precise location of the building within the street, but fortunately the third of these omissions can be filled with the help of other material. The key to the problem is a second Eden Street property, also part of Kingston Canbury manor, to which Portman was admitted at a court of 18th. June 1817 {35}. In a Canbury survey of c.1679 this is described as a copyhold tenement held by Henry and Lydia More and occupied by Nicholas Boxwell {36}. The link with the Mores and a subsequent record of its transfer to George Cole, owner of Hercombe Place, identify the property as the 'tenement late More's' for which Cole and later owners of the mansion paid quit rent to the lords of Kingston manor {37}. The Portman connection, first established in 1768 with the admission of Richard Portman senior, was continued after his death in the following year, first by his daughter Ann Portman, then half a century later (as we have seen) by his son, Richard {38}. Now in his seventies, Richard junior soon disposed of the property, selling it for £750 to Miss Elizabeth Ranyard, a spinster of independent means {39}. She was still the owner when the Tithe Commissioners surveyed Kingston in the late 1830s, and accordingly appears in the apportionment schedule accompanying the Tithe map of 1840. The site of her property (Tithe plot 2025) can be identified with the help of later court records, successive editions of the Ordnance Survey maps and town directories as that now occupied by no. 55 Eden Street {40}.

The relevance of these details for determining the location of the Folly House becomes obvious when we consider a second entry in the Canbury Survey of c.1679. The Folly House is here described, together with an adjacent parcel of orchard ground as a freehold tenancy held of the manor by Robert Warden, formerly by Robert Le Wright, and as lying west of Eden

Street and due north of a brick house occupied by Nicholas Boxwell {41}. The reference to Boxwell is the crucial detail, for it identifies the neighbouring house on the southern side as the Canbury copyhold held by the Mores, and thus locates the Folly site immediately north of plot 2025 on the 1840 Tithe map; this takes us into plot 2024, described in the accompanying apportionment as a house, garden and offices in the occupation of John Dawson. This plot was later occupied by a mansion house called Elm Lawn, which survived into the present century and was only finally demolished in 1938 {43}. It corresponds in the present townscape to the small access way into the rear of Marks and Spencer from Eden Street, and the adjacent office block due north {44}.

1. [**Sampson**, pp. 64-65: M. Vaughan-Lewis in **KUTAS NL** 19 (November 1984).]

2. The enquiry came from E. Rosam of Worcester Park.

3. **Biden**, p. 98, 109.

4. **SRO** 250/6/4.

5. **M&B(Percival)**, vol. IV.

6. Some names from the 1637 map are superimposed in red on the D.O.E./O.S. Royal Parks map of Richmond Park.

7. **KBR** KF1/6/1.

8. **Leland**, vol. IV, p.85 .

9. **Merryweather**, p. 42.

10. [The building is 'le Prison House' in the early seventeenth century, and 'The Folly' appears as an alternative name from c. 1679 onwards: **SRO** 58/1/3/5, f. 4; 58/1/2/4, p. 4; 59/1/1/8.]

11. **KHC** file prints, vol. 11, p. 14 (K1-428); **M&B(Percival)**, vol. V (after p. 406, with a second version in pencil, possibly a rough sketch for the painting, immediately after).

12. [The note may be a later addition: the second part must be if 1779 is the year of execution and the drawing done 'on site'.]

13. [The final part of the note (i.e. from 'called the. . .') is in pencil.]

14. **Biden**, p. 24, note 'p'.

15. **Sampson**, pp. 64-65.

16. **Biden**, p. 24, note 'p' appears to initiate the 'castle' tradition, though it subsequently enjoyed widespread acceptance (see e.g. the nineteenth century O.S. maps which mark the 'site of Warwick's castle'). The Earl of Warwick may have owned land here in the later fifteenth century, as was the local belief in the seventeenth century, but this is a rather different matter: **Aubrey**, vol. I , p. 46.

17. [See above, n. 1.]

18. **Ayliffe**, p.20.

19. **KBR** KG3/2/22, p. 10 (and subsequent Poor Rate lists to 1821, the last in the surviving sequence). He appears in Land Tax books from 1798 to 1813, in which year he purchased redemption: **SRO** QS 6/7. He presumably lived here until his death, aged 80, in 1834: **KPR(Bu)** 25th. October 1834. He is mentioned in **Biden**, p. 24, note 'p'.

20. [House and grounds fill the whole quadrant SW of the junction.]

XX. The Folly, formerly the Prison House in Heathen Street (now Eden Street) 1779. This curious structure stood on the western side of the street just north of what is now the side entrance to Marks and Spencers. (**KHC** file print K1-428).

XXI. The Hand and Mace Public House and Debtors' Prison, sketched by an anonymous artist sometime before 1831. It stood on the north side of what later became Clarence Street on the site now occupied by Bentalls. (**KHC** file print K1-617).

XXII. Gigghill in 1904, looking west from the site of Kingston Post Office. Part of Hodgson's Brewery can be seen on the left, and beyond this the curving facade of the new buildings of c. 1879. now the offices of Bells, solicitors. (**KHC** file print K1-74).

21. **SC** 20th. May 1978.

22. **SRO** 504/1a (8th. December 1781). This implies that the house already existed when Tothill acquired the site from Hemmett's executors, but Biden suggests that Tothill himself built it: **Biden**, p. 24, note 'p'.]

23. [**SRO** 504/1a. The name 'Hercombe Place' occurs in the will of Richard Le Wright (1634) and in Aubrey's late-seventeenth-century account: **PRO** PROB 11/116 (Seagar 112 - p. 375, ii of the **PRO** microfilm); **Aubrey**, vol. I, p. 46. It appears in a corrupt form (*Hestcombes*) in **KBR** KC1/1/145 (of 1653). Memorial brasses of John Hercombe and his wife are in Kingston parish church, and John's will is in **PRO** PROB 11/8 (Millis 11 - p. 93 of **PRO** microfilm).]

24. [For Richard Le Wright's will, see above, n. 23; and for his association with the Earl of Essex, **KPR(B)** 28th. October 1594. His burial is noted in **KPR(Bu)** 8th. December 1634.]

25. Robert Le Wright's baptism is noted in **KPR(B)** 21st. February 1608/09. He was called to the bar on 8th. November 1633: *Register of Admissions to Honourable Society of the Middle Temple*, ed. H. A. C. Sturgess, vol. I (1949).

26. For 'the merchant Cole' see *Rulers of London*, p. 51.

27. Hemmett appears in a Poor Rate list of 1772 apparently in residence, but the house is described as empty in similar lists from 1776 onwards: **KBR** KG3/2/9. He died on 22nd. August 1790, though not it seems at Kingston: **SRO** 504/1a.

28. **KBR** KF1/3/1 etc.

29. See below.

30. M. Vaughan-Lewis in **KUTAS NL** 19 (November 1984).

31. These include several tenements in Norbiton and land in the fields of Kingston: **KBR** KC1/1/143; KC4/3/4 &4/3/6; KC3/3/16 & 3/3/19.

32. For Richard Portman senior, see **KBR** KF1/1/106; KG3/2/9; **SRO** 58/1/2/3, pp. 269, 280. For Richard Portman junior, see below.

33. The elder Portman's death was reported at a Canbury manor court baron on 1st. December 1769. The Folly site and other property in Heathen Street passed to his daughter, Ann : **SRO** 58/1/2/3, p.280.

34. **SRO** 58/1/2/4, p. 10.

35. ibid., p. 110-111 (on the death of Ann Portman).

36. **SRO** 58/1/1/8: descent of title from Mr. & Mrs. Moore to Richard Portman junior can be followed without interruption in the Canbury manor court books (**SRO** 58/1/2/1-4).

37. **SRO** 58/1/2/1; of 15th. October 1689 and recording the surrender to the use of George Cole, Citizen and Merchant of London.

38. **SRO** 58/1/2/3, pp. 268, 280; 58/1/2/4, pp. 110-111.

39. **SRO** 58/1/2/4, p.157 (of 21st. November 1821).

40. i.e. the office block (misleadingly called 'Warwick House') between the access way to the rear of Marks & Spencers and Perrings Furniture store.

41. **SRO** 58/1/1/8.

42. Nicholas Boxall is specifically identified as occupant of the More copyhold: above, n. 36.

43. **SC** 9th. July 1938.

44. ibid: but the report observes that 'the frontage will be set back in connection with the Corporation's planning scheme for the general widening of Eden Street on the side towards the Congregational Church.'

VIII

GIGGHILL IN THE LATE NINETEENTH CENTURY: VICTORIAN TOWN IMPROVEMENTS IN CAMEO

[Earlier papers have shown how civic improvements in the second half of the nineteenth century drastically modified the medieval topography of some parts of Kingston, and how these modifications can often be traced in the formal and initially rather off-putting language of Borough Council Minutes {1}. Another important source for investigating the impact of redevelopment, no less off-putting on first acquaintance, are property deeds. In this short paper, their value is demonstrated with reference to Victorian improvements to that part of the town anciently known as Gigghill (now represented by Eden Street as it approaches the junction with the southern exit from the Market Place) {2}. Discussion is based on a small collection of deeds in the possession of Bells, the firm of local solicitors whose offices are in 'Eagle Chambers', which forms part of this site. They were made available to Miss Wakeford for examination through the initiative of June Sampson in 1983 {3}].

The deeds and other papers in the collection from Bells relate to a block of properties between the former Gigghill passage and the site of Eagle Chambers (which is included) and between Bath Passage and Gigghill itself (now Eden Street). These are now represented by nos. 14 to 18 Eden Street. [Ayliffe gives a good general impression of the character of the area at the time of Queen Victoria's accession.

'Heathen-street, at which is now the end of St. James' road, was exceedingly narrow, tapering off almost to a point. On the site of what is now Eagle Chambers stood Fricker's cooperage which later on became a slaughter-house, and in front of this, separated by a narrow passage, was another old building which in former times had been used as a Presbyterian church. It was a very plain structure with small glass windows at the top. . . . This old building was pulled down in 1836, and the site was thrown into the roadway.
Adjoining the cooperage stood several old wood and gabled houses with very low doorways, entered by two or three steps down. . . . Abutting on these houses was Giggshill passage, which connected Heathen-street with what is now called Bath-passage. It ran down by the side of the premises now occupied by the shop of Freeman, Hardy and Willis. On one side of the passage were cottages occupied by men engaged in the posting work

at the Griffin Hotel; and on the opposite side was Mrs. Chadwick's straw bonnet shop, and a house occupied by one of Kingston's most notable residents at that time, Miss Sally Taylor ' {4}].

The deeds confirm the general accuracy of Ayliffe's description, but also add to it in several ways. In the first place they show that the end of the block, where Eagle Chambers now stands, only became a cooperage in 1816. Earlier it had been occupied by a slaughterhouse and stable or sheep pens, belonging to the Penner family, who were butchers. A slaughterhouse in Gigghill had been acquired by John Penner from Nicholas Boxall (also. a butcher) during the year preceding the Kingston Court Baron of 4th. June 1745 {5}. This is clearly the same property as the quit-rent payable to Kingston manor is 4d. in both 1745 and 1830 {6}. In 1816 this property, with two others in Gigghill was leased by Edward Penner for 21 years to Thomas Fricker, and it was at this point that the slaughterhouse was converted to a cooperage {7}. Thomas Fricker had been apprenticed to a cooper at Cobham in 1803 and was tolerated by Kingston Corporation to trade in the town as a cooper from 1808 {8}. After Fricker's lease expired in 1837, the premises were again used by the Penners as a slaughterhouse, and a *Surrey Comet* leader of 4th. July 1868 referred to the obnoxious small and unsightly appearance of the buildings {9}. It is Penner's slaughterhouse (in effect a reversion to the original use of the site) to which Ayliffe refers. On 15th. January 1864, the owner, a later Edward Penner of Lower Halliford, conveyed the slaughter-house, stable and outbuildings for £350 to Samuel Ranyard Esq., of Claremont Road, Surbiton, who may have been one of the syndicate who had developed St. James's Road *c.* 1858 {10}. Ranyard by this time also owned the six old cottages along Giggshill passage to which Ayliffe alludes, and according to the *Surrey Comet* he offered to let the Corporation have both lots for nothing except the legal costs, so that the passage could be closed and Eden Street widened {11}. The chance was evidently missed, for by a deed of 11th. May 1877 Ranyard sold the cottages and the slaughterhouse, etc., to the Corporation for £800, with the Corporation undertaking to widen and improve that part of Eden Street within two years, under the Kingston Improvement Act of 1855, and so enhance the value of Ranyard's other property there {12}.

Between the two lots of property transferred by Ranyard in 1877, there had been two houses belonging to the Taylor family, probably originally one property (but not Miss Sally Taylor's house mentioned by Ayliffe). The deeds relating to these houses concern leases only, though other documents show that the freehold of the property - now no. 16 Eden Street - came into the hands first of Frederick Sands in 1907, and then in 1933 Page and Bennett {13}. In 1866 the lessee, John Comley, convenanted to demolish the two houses and rebuild by June 1867, but he did not do so {14}. In August 1876 George Imber acquired the balance of the lease and it was stated the houses had been 'pulled down or suffered to fall down'. Imber covenanted to rebuild by the end of 1877, but probably did not {15}. The delays were presumably due to the uncertainty about the Corporation's plans for street-widening, but on 3rd. January 1878 the Corporation acquired Imber's interest in his street frontage of 22 ft. to the depth of about 7 ft., which was thrown into the roadway. The plan in the deed shows the new street-line curving away over the old slaughterhouse site as it now does round Eagle Chambers {16}.

The Eden Street improvements evidently were at last made in 1879. The Corporation demolished the old slaughterhouse buildings (which had more recently been used as a warehouse), widened the street, and then on 6th. February 1879 sold the remainder of this site to James Burgess Boxall of Kingston {17}. Boxall evidently built Eagle Chambers immediately, for he leased certain rooms there to James Thrupp Nightingale for 21 years from 29th. September 1880 {18}. There seems to be no explanation in these documents of the name Eagle Chambers. J.B. Boxall died on 5th. November 1882 and by his will gave the income from this and other property to his widow Margaret Sophie during her widowhood. She died on 24th. November 1890 and under the trusts of her late husband's will, his trustees sold the property on 25th. June 1900 to James Rice Holroyd of Byfleet, miller, for £2,000 {19}. This seems to have been a formality, for the next day Holroyd conveyed it for the same sum to William Edwin Phillips and George Frederick Page (partners in Nightingale, Phillips and Page of Eagle Chambers, auctioneers, surveyors and estate agents). The partners mortgaged it for £1,500 on 2nd. August 1900 to Mrs. Mary Anne Page of Coombe Farm and George Frederick Page of Fassett Road, Kingston {20}.

1. [See above, Papers I & III.]

2. [The name 'Gigghill' occurs as early as 1484: **PNSurrey**, p. 63. No attempt is here made to explain its origins and significance.]

3. [Miss Wakeford produced her own summary of some of the deeds: **KBR** KX79/9. The full collection was listed at **SRO** but no deposit number was given because the material was returned to Bells. Individual items are identified in the following notes either by reference to Miss Wakeford's summaries (**JW** nos. 1, 2 etc.) or by reference to the **SRO** list (**SRO** nos. A1, A2, B1, B2 etc.).]

4. [**Ayliffe**, pp. 22-23.]

5. **KBR** KF1/1/83. [There may be a family connection between this Nicholas Boxall and the Nicholas Boxall who held the More copyhold at the other end of Eden Street: see above, Paper VII, n. 36 & n. 42.]

6. **KBR** KF1/3/21.

7. **SRO** 250/3/75 (part of a separate sequence of deeds relating to this area).

8. **SRO** 250/3/4-5.

9. **SC** 4th. July 1868.

10. **Merryweather**, pp. 44-45.

11. **SC** 4th. July 1868.

12. Bells Deeds (**JW** no.6; **SRO** no. A3).

13. *ibid*. (**JW** no. 14; **SRO** no. A12).

14. *ibid*. (**SRO** no. B14).   15. *ibid*. (**SRO** no. B16).

16. *ibid*. (**SRO** no. B17).   17. *ibid*. (**SRO** no. A6).

18. *ibid*. (**JW** no. 10; **SRO** no. A7).   19. *ibid*. (**JW** no. 12; **SRO** no. A7).

20. *ibid*. (**JW** no. 12; **SRO** no. A9).

PART II:

SOME KINGSTON BUILDINGS
PAST AND PRESENT

XXIII. The new bridge across the Thames at the time of the Great Frost of 1895. The vagaries of the climate posed a much greater problem with regard to maintaining its wooden predecessor. (**KHC** file print K1-138).

XXIV. Floods in Kingston High Street, 1895. An awesome reminder of the power of the Thames to disrupt the town's life, even in an age of industrial and technological progress. (**KHC** file print K1-862).

IX

FINANCING PUBLIC BUILDING IN EARLY KINGSTON : TWO CASE STUDIES

[Apart from its parish church, Kingston's public buildings were of no great size or exceptional architectural merit before the nineteenth century, though this should not be taken as a criticism of the old unreformed Corporation but rather as a comment on contemporary views about what local authorities were expected to achieve. Quite simply, our ancestors would have been surprised, perhaps even alarmed by the suggestion that elaborate and costly programmes of civic improvement should have been a regular concern of their rulers {1}. Nor, had Kingston Corporation wished to alter expectations, would it easily have found the means to do so, for by modern standards local public finance at the time was ramshackled and hand-to-mouth. The prevailing situation is well illustrated in the two items making up this paper. 'Maintaining the Great Bridge' was written in 1972, with substantial amendments ten years later, and 'Paying for Queen Anne's Statue' in May 1975. Both were found among Miss Wakeford's papers and reflect her long-standing interest in the practical workings of local government in early Kingston {2}. This interest achieved a more substantial expression in a study entitled 'The Administration of Kingston upon Thames, Surrey, in the Early Eighteenth century', submitted as part of her work for the University of London Extra-Mural Diploma in History in 1956/57. It remains unpublished, but is (to my knowledge) the only detailed examination of its subject yet made {3}.]

Maintaining the Great Bridge

Surviving documents tell us a good deal about the problem of maintaining the Great Bridge from late-medieval times onwards. It seems clear that the bridge piers in the river and the carriageway over it were always of wood, as in the nineteenth century, but there is no (documentary) indication before the 1580s of the nature of the footings on land {4}. The bridge seems to have been so frail that one assumes it was almost wholly wooden in early times. It was vulnerable not only to floods but also in times of civil disturbance to deliberate damage by those who wished to deny its use to their enemies. For example, in 1308 Edward II ordered the destruction of the bridge and then gave the town £10 for its repair. 'Destruction' may have meant only the careful removal of a length of, say, 30 feet over the river (as was done by the men of Kingston in 1554 to delay Wyatt in his rising against Queen Mary) {5}. Deliberate damage of this sort was probably easy enough to repair;

43

destruction by natural forces was likely to be more drastic and there seem to have been three periods of real disaster. In each case we are reminded forcefully of the extensive damage that could quickly follow from sudden rises in the river levels, and of the resulting strain which this placed on public finances.

The first period of disaster was in the early-thirteenth century. There was a great tempest in 1222, recorded because the tower of Merton Priory was blown down. There is no direct record of its effects in Kingston, but there is evidence of disastrous floods here at about this time and in 1223 Henry III entrusted 'the work of the bridge' to Henry de St. Albans and a local merchant called Matthew, son of Geoffrey. The bridge is described on this occasion as 'destitute of all help, aid and skill', and the king ordered possession of the house with which the structure had earlier been endowed, and its other assets to be given over to one of the two men {6}. The appointment by the king indicates something out of the ordinary and the work must have been very substantial, possibly even a complete rebuilding. It may be that it was at this time that the lower site referred to by Leland was abandoned and the bridge re-sited where it remained till the nineteenth century. This would give good time for the development of the houses on the northern side of Old Bridge Street that are mentioned in the deed of 1360 {7}.

Throughout the thirteenth and fourteenth centuries there are scattered references to damage suffered by the Great Bridge from natural causes. It was affected by heavy flooding in the 1250s, 1260s and 1280s, and by severe winters in 1269 and 1281: and in an interesting letter sent to Edward I from Gascony to his regent in England in 1286, it is described as (or as having recently been) unusable {8}. During the fourteenth century there were several grants of pontage (the right to charge tolls on goods passing over and beneath the bridge) for fixed periods by the crown, some of which specifically mention the ailing condition of the structure {9}. The problem seems to have reached crisis proportions towards the end of the century . A grant of pontage in 1376 describes the bridge as 'broken down', a second grant in 1383 was probably necessitated by abnormal flooding of the Thames between Windsor and Westminster in the previous year, and a third grant in 1400 was accompanied by the appointment of three men, probably all royal officials, to collect the moneys and oversee the repairs. The fact that one of them was the famous master carpenter, Hugh Herland, who was responsible at this time for the timber roof of Westminster Hall, indicates that important work in timber was involved {10}. It may have been some time before the difficulties were overcome, for Henry IV made a further grant of pontage in 1406/8 {11}.

The third spell of natural disaster came towards the end of the sixteenth century. Bridgewardens' accounts have survived from this century and many of them give interesting details of the daily expenditure on materials and labour {12}. The earlier accounts show constant repairs to the bridge and there is little indication that anything but timber was used for the structure. In 1531, for example, the wardens paid 2s. 4d. for two loads of timber 'to make *sumeras* for the brydge', and in the next year they paid 10d for a load of stones 'for the hunder pynnynge of the *somer* of the bridge' {13}. In 1541 they bought six loads of stones for the bridge for 5s., and three men brought two of the loads each from Shene (Richmond). In the same year a man was paid 5d. for digging away the earth from the piles. It looks therefore as though this was more broken stone being brought in to strengthen the foundations, not for the structure. The stone was bought from Edward, Earl of Hertford, who in 1540 had been granted the site of the suppressed Carthusian Priory of Shene (founded by Henry V in 1414); it may well have been worked stone from this building. In 1543 the wardens bought ten loads of piles and *sommers*, but the material is not stated. In 1544 they paid 4d. 'for mending the iron of the high peer'. The cost of spreading gravel on the bridge and causeway is often mentioned. When substantial timber repairs were undertaken, the timber arrived by river and was laid on the Bull wharf, and sawpits were made there (on at least one occasion by the gravedigger !) {14}. The accounts have interesting details of the repair or making of tools, wheelbarrows and machinery for the work including gynnes and rams {15}. There are payments to watermen for rescuing the bridge timbers from the river in time of flood and (usually for only a few weeks at a time), to a ferryman for a horse-boat, presumably when the bridge was unsafe for wheeled traffic. In the sixteenth century Bull wharf was not paved (a man was paid to beat down the earth in the yard when some bridge work was finished), and in the seventeenth century leases of the site granted by the corporation the trees are specifically reserved {16}.

Although repairs to the bridge are a constant theme of the accounts throughout the sixteenth century, problems seems to have increased significantly in the final decades of Elizabeth I's reign. Very extensive work became necessary in or about 1585, and although the structure was evidently stable again by the following year when 6d. was paid to 'certain women for bringing sedge and flags against the Queen's coming over to Hampton Court', new difficulties were evidently caused in December 1587 by the bad winter weather that hampered Drake in his efforts against the gathering Spanish Armada. There were extensive repairs to the existing bridge throughout the year ending Michaelmas 1588, perhaps in the nature of first-aid. In the following year a ferry was in use, and we also find the first mention of a mason who was paid 4s. 'for 3 days coming hither and one day going to London'. His presence suggests that major building work was clearly in stone. Ashlar stone was bought at the quarry and conveyed to London by land and water, and then craned out of the ship into barges and brought up to Kingston. More stone was bought in 1591. The payments for materials and labour go on for some years and in 1596/97 there is one 'to Abraham for going into Kent for the stones', apparently the only reference to the provenance of the stone {17}.

This re-building in the 1590s was almost certainly the last major structural work on the bridge, though it was often in disrepair in later years. The third book of Bridgewardens' accounts, covering the period 1604-1708 is less useful as a guide to structural problems, since the entries usually give the names of persons paid rather than details of the nature of the work done or material supplied {18}. However, it is possible to identify from them a number of periods of special difficulty. One was 1607/8 when the Thames was frozen over and the bridge broken down. Another was 1703 when the famous 'Great Storm' in November not only destroyed the spire of Kingston church but also damaged the bridge. As a consequence £ 150 had to be raised on mortgage of Bridge property to meet the costs of repairs. In 1774, a further mortgage was necessary following exceptionally high floods, the levels of which can still be observed in marks on the wall of Twickenham church. In 1822 there was a further great flood, said to have been four inches higher than in 1774 in some places, and it was as a direct consequence of this latest innundation that the decision to rebuild Kingston Bridge in stone on its present site was taken. The new bridge was opened in 1827, and its timber predecessor dismantled, the materials being sold off at public auction {19}.

There are several guides to the physical appearance of the old bridge in its later years. John Aubrey describes it in about 1673 as having twenty interstices, two in the middle wide enough for barges to pass through, and twenty-two piers of wood supporting it, containing 126 yards 'besides at the east end 30 yards wrought up of stone and brick, and at the west end 12 yards'. He also mentions in the middle of the bridge two fair seats for passengers to avoid carts and to sit and enjoy 'the delightful prospect' {20}. In addition, there are several well-known sketches of the bridge, some of which have appeared in modern publications {21}. To those of us weaned on the wonders of twentieth century technology, the structure appears both crude and flimsy, and so it undoubtedly was: but for those charged with the responsibility of maintaining the bridge, it was a major drain on their time, energy and scarce resources. The remarkable thing is that they were able to meet that responsibility, albeit with great difficulty, for as long as they did.

Paying for Queen Anne's Statue

Now that the question of local rates is so much to the fore, it is especially interesting to read of Kingston Corporation's great financial undertaking of 1706, when the old Guildhall was restored and graced with the gilded statue of Queen Anne which now looks over the Market Place from the nineteenth century Town Hall {22}. The Guildhall, seen in Rowlandson's and other drawings, and in the centre of Hornor's map, was probably built after the 1481 charter, which granted the town its incorporation and the right to hold the Saturday Court before its bailiffs and steward {23}. After this, one building evidently served as both Guildhall and Court Hall. A deed of 1505 in the Borough records refers to a shop under 'le new Corte Hall', suggesting that it was also used in part for economic purposes {24}. A building of about 1500 would have been timber-framed and by 1700 old-fashioned and perhaps in poor condition. At the end of November 1703 the town was hit by the famous 'Great Storm' which did over £2 million worth of damage in London alone and sank twelve warships within sight of land. The steeple of Kingston church was destroyed and there must have been much damage in the town {25}. This was probably the reason why the Corporation in November 1704 ordered that the Court Hall and the Stockhouse (the town gaol) should be repaired {26}. Soon afterwards they decided to enlarge and furnish one of the rooms in the Hall to make it suitable for corporation meetings and other municipal business and to provide there two fire-places, with another in the room underneath for the constables and watch {27}. Evidently once they embarked on this work they found that they would also have to do something about the large room where the Assize judges sat and on 21st. February 1705/06 the Corporation unanimously agreed that this (the southern) part of

46

the Court Hall should be pulled down and rebuilt in the fashionable brick {28}. The resulting structure was a curious hybrid: the medieval style of the first-floor room supported on timber posts over an open space was retained (for the sake, presumably, of the rent from the shops) but the posts were replaced by wooden Grecian columns (brought up the river from London) and a vaguely flemish gable, on which a sundial was later set, was also added. This sat between the Tudor pitched roofs, and a rounded embrasure was made in the centre of the building for the Queen's statue.

The growing scope of these plans immediately raised financial problems, Kingston Corporation had no power to levy rates and its legal capacity to hold land (then almost the only form of investment) had been limited by the 1628 charter to an annual value of £100 {29}. There was no forward budgeting and there were no salaried officers. The members of the Court of Assembly (or as we should say, town councillors) took turns to serve the various offices, rather as councillors now act as chairmen of committees. Two chamberlains had somewhat the function of borough treasurer: they had to receive the income of the 'Chamber', lay it out as instructed by the Court of Assembly and at Michaelmas present an account, supported by receipts, showing precisely how they had spent the money and what was in hand or owing to them. The accounts were audited by a specially appointed sub-committee of the Corporation . Thus the shrewd tradesmen of Kingston kept an eye on each other. The Corporation's orders about rebuilding were directed to the Chamberlains, and in particular to the senior of them, Mr. John Banford, a master blacksmith. A Mr. Yeomans of Hampton was to be consulted about the drawings and design for the new court room (his fee was £1 4s. 0d.) and not more than 2s. a day was to be paid to the carpenters and bricklayers. The Bailiffs and four other members were to inspect the work from time to time, but it was for Mr. Banford to manage the operation, to purchase materials and arrange for their transport to the site and engage the labour, paying out of his own pocket if there was no money in the Chamber {30}.

Meanwhile the Corporation was trying various experiments to raise the necessary capital. The old wood, iron and even glass was sold for £3 18s. 6d., the great bell-metal pot in the Court Hall for £2 17s. 6d. (at 9d. per pound). Two hundred and fifteen trees belonging to the Corporation were felled and sold for £50 and the sum earmarked for the work on the Court Hall. The pest house built during the plague of the 1590s was little used now that the scourge had died out, so the site, which was well outside the town, where Dudley Road now is, was sold for 20 guineas, The pest house itself was sold to Smith's Gift, the wealthiest of the local charities, and re-erected in the Horse Fair 'for a house to imploy the poor to work in' -- Kingston's first workhouse {31}. A Twickenham house painter was 'tolerated' to exercise his trade in the town on condition that he did £10 worth of painting for the Corporation {32}. Even the £1 1s. 0d. paid for permission to land goods on the Corporation's wharf was ordered to be paid towards the rebuilding of the Court Hall {33}. With all these efforts the Corporation could still not keep up with the costs and in April 1706 one of the Bailiffs lent the Chamberlain 20 guineas to go on with, repayable out of the first moneys to come in. But the unfortunate Chamberlain, who had been £23 out of pocket by Michaelmas 1705, was £51 down a year later. The Court of Assembly then

47

ordered that he should be reimbursed by the Chamber all sums which he should be out of pocket in building the Court Hall and making the gilding of the Queen's Effigies {34}. At the same time they ordered a gold inscription under the Queen's picture recording that it had been painted and given by Sir Godfrey Kneller in 1706. There had not in fact been any previous order to provide a statue, and it may be that the Court of Assembly, while (unusually) allowing him interest at 6% on the moneys which he had had to advance, ordered that he should not expend above 20s. on any extraordinary occasion without an order from the Corporation {35}. Following his orders, he spent £7 17s. 0d. in buying and bringing up from London 24 Russian leather chairs, 12s. 6d. for an oval table and £14 14s. 0d. on hangings and a carpet. He paid Mr. Bird £47 18s. 6d. for the Queen's statue and the waterman 1s. 6d. for bringing up the painting and 10s. 6d. for the carriage of the picture frame and pedestal. Tips of £2 3s. 0d. to 'Sir Godfrey Kneller's Gentleman' and 10s. 0d. 'to the other servants' seem large by comparison. Altogether £400 was spent on the rebuilding and refurnishing and £200 of this had to be met by mortgaging the Corporation's lands to Mr. Henry Winder, the Master of the Grammar School. Some years later, when he wanted his money back, the mortgage was assigned to Mr. Yeomans, the surveyor originally consulted {36}.

Mr. Banford must have been well pleased when his efforts culminated in a 'rearing dinner' to celebrate the raising of the Queen's statue into her commanding position, 14s. was spent at the Bull in Thames Street and 15s. 10d. laid out on beef, a leg of veal, bacon, butter and tobacco for the feast. One Mrs. Wray received £1 17s. 0d. 'for dressing the rearing Dinner and bear (i.e. beer) then and other things', and finally Mr. Banford was given an honorarium of £6 0s. 0d. 'for his pains and care in looking after ye workmen yt built ye Court Hall'. He must have earned it {37}.

1. [For general background, see G. Martin, 'The Town as Palimpsest' in *The Study of Urban History*, ed. H. J. Dyos, (1968), pp. 155-169.]

2. [**KBR** KX79/34; 79/58; 79/59.]

3. [I have been unable to find a copy of this work among Miss Wakeford's papers in KBR, but the University of London presumably holds the original.]

4. [Recent excavations on the bridge site will doubtless throw new light on these matters.]

5. J. R. Maddicott, *Thomas of Lancaster*, (1970), p. 78: **VCH Surrey**, vol. III pp. 488-489.

6. *ibid.*

7. [See above, Paper II.].

8. Details of weather and flooding are taken from J. H. Brazell, *London Weather*, H.M.S.O., (1968). Edward I's letter was first drawn to local notice by Dr. Taylor whose translation (from **PRO** C47, 34/4, no. 33) appeared in *Kingston Tower* (the parish magazine of All Saints) in 1953. I am grateful to Dr. Taylor for supplying me with a transcription. [See also **KUTAS NL** 12 (May 1982).]

9. By Edward II in 1318 (for six years), Edward III in 1376 (for ten years) and Richard II in 1383 (for five years): **VCH Surrey**, vol III, p.489.

10. ibid. The 1400 grant was for three years and Herland's fellow commissioners were William Loveney and Richard Keys.

XXV. The Old Court Hall in the Market Place with its statue of Queen Anne, 1830. Within a few years, it was to be replaced by the Market Hall which still stands today. (**KHC** file print K1-550).

XXVI. The rear of the Old Court Hall sketched from the north-east corner of the Market Place c.1700. (**KHC** file print K1-1189).

XXVII. The Rowbarge at the western end of Old Bridge Street c.1895. Its Edwardian replacement survived until the recent redevelopment of the area. (**KHC** file print K1-215).

11. Again for three years.

12. **KBR** KB18/3/1; 18/3/2. The first volume (covering 1527-47 and 1565-67) has been edited as **SRS** vol XXII (1955) and there is a transcription of the second (covering 1568-1603) in **KHC.** [References to these sources in subsequent paragraphs are not individually footnoted.]

13. *Sumeras* (Eng. 'sommers' or 'somers') are the main beams in any substantial timber structure.

14. For the Bull Wharf see **KBR** KC1/1/114-119.

15. For technical background see L. F. Salzman, *Building in England before 1540*, (2nd. ed., 1967), pp. 318-29.

16. **KBR** KC1/1/114-118.

17. For costs of ashlar see Salzman, *op. cit.* (above n.15), pp.103-104.

18. **KBR** KB18/3/3.

19. For the new bridge, see **Sampson**, pp. 105-106.

20. **Aubrey**, vol I, pp. 45-46.

21. The old and new bridges appear together in a sketch of c.1827 in **Sampson**, opposite p. 35.

22. [The current debate on the proposed Poll Tax lends yet greater point to this comment.]

23. For Rowlandson's sketch see **KHC** file prints, vol. 2, p. 16 (K1-939); vol. 6, p. 27 (K1-3187); vol 8, p. 19 (K1-3186). Drawings of the Market Place by Grosse (1770) and an anonymous eighteenth-century artist are in **Sampson**, opposite pp. 51 & 83. The 1481 charter is **KBR** KA1/15.

24. **KBR** KC1/1/87.

25. **Sampson**, p.93.

26. **KBR** KB1/1, p. 333.

27. *ibid.,* p.340.

28. *ibid.,* p.351.

29. **KBR** KA1/27.

30. Banford's accounts for the period are in **KBR** KD5/l/2. [References to this source in subsequent paragraphs are not individually footnoted.]

31. **KBR** KB1/1, pp. 343, 347, 353. The 'new' poor house lasted until 1742 (**KBR** KB1/2, p. 71.

32. **KBR** KB1/1, p. 351 (the painter was William Redding).

33. *ibid.,* p. 354.

34. *ibid.,* p. 359.

35. *ibid.,* p. 368.

36. *ibid.,* p. 357.

37. Details of the Bull Inn at this time are discussed by P. Hodges in **KUTAS NL** 12 (May 1982).

X

SOME NOTES ON A QUARTET OF KINGSTON ALEHOUSES

[The importance of brewing in the economy of early modern Kingston has long been recognised, although its role remains to be examined in detail. Recently, however, there has been a surge of interest in one particular side of the industry - the increasing numbers of inns and alehouses that collectively provided the physical setting for the retailing trade {1}. The present paper brings into focus four of Kingston's more modest drinking establishments, This type of building lacked the complex socio-economic functions of large inns like 'The Castle' and 'The Sun', but existed in greater numbers and drew its clientele from a wider social spectrum: its position within the general picture cannot therefore be dismissed as insignificant {2}. 'The Three Coneys' first appeared in KUTAS NL for February 1977, the remainder, all dated October/November 1980 and found among Miss Wakeford's papers, were drafted in connection with the publication mentioned under note 1, below. Miss Wakeford's working notes contain a substantial file on local inns and alehouses and the local brewing industry in general, but most of this material is unfortunately not in a form suitable for publication {3}.]

The Old Crown (Church Street)

'The Old Crown' in Church Street, formerly London Street, and earlier still King Street, was called 'The Chequer' until the eighteenth century. The earliest reference I have traced so far is in a rental of the manor of Kingston for half of 1417 {4}. At this time the owner, Juliana Whetle, living in High Row, was paying 10³/4d. half-yearly (1s. 9¹/2d. per annum) for 'a tenement and the Cheker and 3 posts (*postibus*) in King Street'. The posts may have been hitching and/or sign posts. The rent was a fixed manorial quit-rent, not a lease-rent of the modern type and was payable to Kingston Corporation, which stood in place of the King as the lord of the manor of Kingston. Later quit-rentals have not survived until 1708 when the owner was paying 1s. 4d. per annum for the property {5}. This would suggest that 5¹/2d. of the original 1s. 9¹/2d. annual quit rent was for the three posts, and that some time before the eighteenth century the posts had been taken into the adjacent street, leading to a downward adjustment of the rent.

In Tudor times, and probably much earlier, the establishment had a well, for in Kingston Parish Register there is an entry for 24th. June 1597 that Christopher Atkynson (a master builder according to Apprenticeship records) was found drowned 'in the cheker well and was bered' {6}. By this time the building may have been very old, for in 1605 an orchard on the far side of what is now Union Street was referred to as belonging to 'a decayed tenement called the chequer' {7}. It was evidently rebuilt and in use by 1648 however, for in that year a lease of a stable and garden belonging to it was assigned to Richard Rose, a miller who owned a windmill in Canbury Field {8}. Rose also acquired the Chequer itself, for when he died in 1657, he bequeathed it to his son, also Richard. It later became the property of Henry Paine in the right of his wife, Anne, a member of the Rose family {9}. Paine himself was a member of one of those Kingston families who were vintners and citizens of London and among whom there were various inter-marriages in the seventeenth century. In 1705 Paine sold the Chequer to Stephen Cole of Twickenham and according to the manorial quit-rent rolls, a Stephen Cole still owned it in 1764 {10}. By 1776 it was owned by the brewer John Rowlls and like many other pubs owned by this family, it later passed to the brewers Hodgsons, and then to Courages. Certainly from the seventeenth century (and also in 1417 and probably later) the licensees were tenants not owners. One of them, Daniel Smith, victualler, was fined at the Kingston Court leet of 29th. May 1705 for not scouring two rod of common sewer near the Queen's highway behind the Chequer {11}. This would have been an open drainage ditch for surface water running along what is now Union Street.

The seventeenth century rebuilt Chequer was a timber-framed building in which material from the earlier inn was probably used, and substantial portions of this structure can still be seen from the Union Street side {12}. About 1722 the front of the Stuart building was rebuilt in the fashionable red brick, giving the present early-Georgian appearance. As the new front encroached on the street (i.e. on the waste of Kingston manor) the Corporation as manorial lords granted a 99-year lease dated 14th. February 1722/23 at an annual rent of 4s. of a piece of waste land along the front, 40 ft. long and 2 ft. wide {13}. The inn was still called 'The Chequer' at this point, but by 1764 had been renamed 'The Horse and Groom'. When acquired by John Rowlls the name was changed again to 'The Crown'. For a time in the early nineteenth century it became 'The Bull and Butcher' (being close to the east side of the Market Place where there were many butchers), but by 1819 was 'The Old Crown'. Ayliffe gives a brief account of the inn in 1837 {14}.

The Rowbarge (Old Bridge Street) {15}

The site seems to have had two houses on it when it was sold by the Corporation in 1620 to Nathaniel Nicholles, who had served his apprenticeship as a draper and was thus free to trade in Kingston {16}. The Corporation reserved an annual rent of 40s. on this occasion, thereafter included in the Chamberlains' Accounts: thus successive owners and usually the tenants too can be readily identified {17}. Early entries in the accounts refer to 'two tenements near the Great Bridge', but by the end of the seventeenth century the property is identified as 'a tenement in Thames Street', suggesting that the two houses of 1620 had been rebuilt as one {18}. The name 'Rowbarge' appears in the Chamberlains' Account for 1706 in connection with arrears of rent payable to the Corporation for 1699, but it is not immediately apparent how long before this the building had functioned as an alehouse {19}. Henry Pembrook, who paid the 40s. rent from about 1629, was at 'The Dolphin' in 1639, so may have commenced his career as a licensee at the Rowbarge {20}. In 1674 when the tenant was Richard Jones, the building was assessed to Hearth Tax for four hearths, indicating a modest establishment {21}. According to the 1705 Watch List in the first Bailiffs' Minute Book, Richard Hancock was then the tenant, and he was licensed for an alehouse keeper by the Kingston Justices at their session of 23rd. February 1707/08, the first session recorded in the same book {22}. In the eighteenth century, the licensees may be traced in the licencing sessions of the Kingston Justices and in the Poor Rate books {23}. The Rowbarge was acquired by the Rowlls family in the second half of the eighteenth century, sold to W.F. Hodgson in 1854 and in 1886 taken over by Hodgson's Kingston Brewery, who rebuilt it in about 1900 {24}. Recently demolished, the c.1900 building was an interesting example of the architecture of Hodgson's late Victorian town public houses, and as such deserved to be recorded. Of the physical characteristics of its predecessor, we know little at present, though there are several old photographs in Kingston Heritage Centre of the exterior, and Ayliffe describes it as 'a very low ancient building . . . .(where) the shopkeepers of the town would assemble to chat, sip their grog and play whist, and discuss municipal affairs' {25}.

The Three Coneys (London Road)

Dr. Finny and others had recorded a halfpenny trade token showing three rabbits, issued in 1669 by Robert Pearson of Kingston {26}. This device had sometimes been interpreted as the sign of a furrier . (The rabbits do not however appear in the arms of the furriers' livery company, the Skinners Company of London, and the Company has not confirmed that they were used as a sign). Kingston Borough records refer to premises called 'The Three Coneys', and as coney was the old word for rabbit, it seemed likely that the token belonged to an alehouse of that name. The Three Coneys was in Norbiton and appeared from the rate books to be on the Fairfield side of the present London Road (earlier Norbiton Street) but its precise location was not known. Recently, copies of documents relating to No. 30 London Road (the Oxfam shop), kindly supplied by the present owner, have shown that the property had formerly been known as the Three Coneys, and this has enabled us at last to link the various pieces of information available in local records. In addition the present tenants kindly permitted an internal examination of the building {27}.

The building is a brick-built house of two main floors, plus cellar and attics {28}. It has a front and a rear room on each floor, with a central stairway between them. There is a chimney in each section, but it seems likely that originally only the two ground-floor rooms had fireplaces. The single-floor extension at the back is modern, as are the windows in the main building. A particularly interesting point is that the field-bricks of which the house is built appear identical with those used for the nearby Cleave's Almshouses, built in 1669/70. For this and other reasons, the house has been dated to the third quarter of the seventeenth century and the documentary evidence supports this very well. The trade token is dated 1669, but Robert Pearson (more usually spelt Peirson) is shown in the Hearth Tax assessments of 1664 and 1674 as occupying a house with two hearths in just about this spot {29}. James King of Kingston master tailor, buried in All Saints' church on 26th. March 1674, is the earliest owner traced (occupiers not owners are listed in the Hearth Tax returns) and may have had the Three Coneys built {30}. The later owners can be followed in the court rolls of the Corporation's manor of Kingston, to which they paid an annual quit-rent of 11d., but as they never occupied the house, the tenants have proved more interesting {31}.

The Peirson family, the earliest tenants, have been traced back in Kingston Parish Registers to the beginning of the seventeenth century {32}. Successive generations were bricklayers, living near others of the same trade in the London Road/Cambridge Road area {33}. It seems likely that they built their own small houses (of which only the Three Coneys survives), and also the Almshouses. Four generations of the Peirson family, all with eldest sons named Robert, lived at the Three Coneys. Robert I, born in 1612, was buried in Kingston in 1673 and was then described as bricklayer 'from the Cunneys' {34}. Robert II (1635-1680), bricklayer, was probably the one who issued the trade token in 1669 {35}. On Robert III (1660-1724) there is more information. He was a victualler (i.e. a publican) and in 1700 he was appointed Cryer to the Court of Kingston, a profitable office which he held until his death {36}. There are very few rate assessments for the early eighteenth century, but it seems that he had left the Three Coneys by 1705 {37}. His son Robert was too young to take it on and in 1703 was apprenticed to a butcher {38}. As Cryer to the Court, Robert III acted for the Recorder, bailiffs, and magistrates, by serving writs and summonses, collecting fines, crying the triple 'Oyez' to open court proceedings, reading the 'charge' to juries, etc. He also had to keep an account of the quit-rents and tolls, which were the perquisite of the bailiffs, and probably collected the former. The Cryer was paid by fees for the individual duties, and perhaps also by commission on the rents collected. The rolls of the Skinners' Company are not among those in the Guildhall Library of the City of London, but the Company's Beadle, Mr. J.W. Cross, very kindly searched their records and extracted the (fairly common) names of various Kings and Peirsons who were members between 1593 and 1675. It has not proved possible to associate any of them with the Kingston families, but there may be some connection. No other explanation of the name the Three Coneys has appeared.

The building evidently ceased to be an alehouse, probably before the middle of the eighteenth century, and was later occupied in connection with small holdings of land in the Fairfield and further along Norbiton Street. In the early nineteenth century, the tenants were the Day family, who had a nursery garden and florist's business in London Road until fairly recent times. Though now a small and unremarkable building, with modern windows, the former Three Coneys may well be the earliest brick-built house now surviving in the old borough of Kingston. As Kingston was using bricks for domestic buildings relatively early for south-east England, it is unfortunate that so little early brickwork is left {39}.

A Postscript {40}

An indication of the level of prosperity that could be enjoyed by builders at a time when brick was becoming fashionable is given by the following extracts from the will of Anne Peirson. Anne, who made her will on 1st. November 1695 and died soon afterwards, was the widow of William Peirson, a master bricklayer (in modern terms a builder) who had been bailiff of Kingston and lived in Norbiton, probably in the street now called London Road. He was the younger brother of Robert I, tenant of the Three Coneys, and was buried in Kingston on 5th. May 1695 {41}. By his will of 9th. July 1690 he left his residuary personal estate to his widow, who continued to live in the same house. He owned four houses in Kingston, and his comfortable economic position is reflected in his widow's evident pride in her household goods. Pewter tableware was usual at this time among such people as the successful tradesmen of Kingston, and her six leather chairs must also have been a status symbol {42}. The specific bequests made in Mrs. Peirson's will included:
'My bedd in the best Chamber and all the Furniture belonging to it with the window curtaines in the same Chamber'.
'One silver spoon, one paire of flaxen sheetes and pillow bears (i.e. pillow cases), one Table cloth, one dozen of napkins'.
'One paire of Holland Sheetes and pillowbeares, alsoe my wedding Ring and an old piece of Gold that shall be found with it'.
'One long Diaper Tablecloath, one Cupboard Cloath, one dozen of diaper Napkins, one paire of Flaxen Sheetes'.
'The Table and Stooles and half a dozen of Leather Chaires that are in the Parlour, and my Chest of Drawers in the Chamber over the Parlour, and the greates of my brasse Kettles'.
'The least of my brasse Kettles, two brass skilletts, a brass mortar and pessell'.
'Half a dozen of pewter dishes, two pewter quart potts'.
'One brasse pott, two brasse Candlesticks, one pewter Flagon'.
'My bedd in the Garrett with all belonging to it and one paire of Sheetes and pillowbeares, one Tablecloath, half a dozen Napkins'.
'One paire of Flaxen Sheetes, one paire of Pillowbeares, one Tablecloath, half a dozen of napkins'.
'Half a dozen of my biggest pewter dishes'.

The George and Dragon (Kingston Hill)

The George and Dragon, Kingston Hill, recently transformed into the prestigious Kingston Lodge Hotel, was formerly called The George, and earlier still The Fox and Coney. The land on which successive buildings stood belonged to the Cleave Almshouse Charity and was transferred to the trustees of Kingston Municipal Charities in 1893, when W.F. Hodgson was the lessee. The site was part of two acres of land on the south side of London Lane owned by John Evelyn and his son George before 1605, and by 1624 (when there was apparently a house on the land) belonged to Thomas Tiffyn and his wife, Grace {43}. The Tiffyns were brewers and it may be that they established the alehouse at this time {44}. The land was on the edge of

XXVIII. The Rose and Crown at the eastern end of Old Bridge Street on the eve of its
destruction c.1900. Demolition first brought to light the fourteenth- century vaulted
undercroft whose recent rediscovery has attracted so much interest in the town. (**KHC**
file print K1-379).

XXIX.   The Dolphin Inn at the turn of the century. Its buildings originally stretched
from the Horse Fair to the Church Yard, but were severely curtailed with the creation of
Clarence Street. (**SC** 20C 638).

XXX.   The George & Dragon, Kingston Hill, 1932. Formerly called the Fox and Coney,
the early fortunes of this hostelry owed much to the crowds who attended public
executions at the nearby town gallows. (**KHC** file print K1-3194).

Coombe Warren and was leased in 1695 to Robert Arnold, warrener, and in 1724 to his widow, Susanna {45}. Robert Arnold is in a list of persons licensed by the Kingston Justices on 23rd. February 1707/08 to keep an alehouse {46}. The alehouse, under its former name of the Fox and Coney is referred to on the last page of *The Kingston Atalantis or Woodward's Miscellany* in a satirical letter dated 31st. May 1729 concerning the leasing of Corporation waste land on Kingston Hill {47}. Evidently inspired by a lease of 20th. February 1728 to a butcher, Nathaniel Hammond, the letter refers to building 'a house or two to entertain Spectators at the Executions' {48}. As the gallows was nearby, it may be assumed that the Fox and Coney also gained business from the public hangings {49}. From 1724 the Corporation leases of the alehouse are entered in the Kingston Ledger, and in 1748 the premises were leased for the first time to John Rowlls the brewer, who had acquired the brewery in Eden Street (then Heathen Street) in 1745 {50}. From this time the lessees were the Rowlls family and their successors Hodgsons, and later Courages. In 1779 the alehouse was called The George, a name which was still in use in 1893, but soon afterwards it appears in a local directory as the George and Dragon {51}. Possibly the new name was associated with a rebuilding, for the structure incorporated into the new Hotel apparently dates from the later nineteenth century.

1. [See, e.g., *Local Inns and Hotels (Photographs from the Local Illustrations Collection of Kingston upon Thames Heritage Unit)*, ed. C. A. Cornish (Royal Borough of Kingston upon Thames Recreation Department, s.d.).]

2. [For general background, see A. Everitt, 'The English Urban Inn 1560-1760' in *Perspectives in English Urban History*, ed. A. Everitt, (1973), pp. 91-137.]

3. **[KBR KX72/1/2; KX79/48.]**

4. **KBR KD4/2.**

5. **KBR KF1/3/1.**

6. **KPR(Bu)** 24th. June 1597: **Apprentices**, nos. 93 & 1591.

7. **KBR KC1/1/134.**

8. Minet Library, deed no 745.

9. **SRO** 212/64/19.

10. **KBR KF1/1/49; KF1/3/2; 1/3/4.**

11. **KBR KF1/1/49.**

12. Information from Mr. I. J. West.

13. **KBR KC1/1/141.**

14. **Ayliffe**, p. 28.

15. [The building has recently been demolished as part of the Horsefair re-development programme.]

16. **KBR KC1/1/79.**

17. **KBR KD5/1/1** (from p. 397 onwards); 5/1/2.

18. **KBR KD5/1/1.**

19. **KBR KD5/1/2.**

20. **KBR** KD5/1/1: **SRO** 212/64/11.

21. **PRO** 179/188/496.

22. **KBR** KE2/5/1, f. 3a.

23. There is a separate record for 1828-96, i.e. **KBR** KD2/6/1.

24. For early photographs see **KHC** file prints, vol. 2, p. 39 (K1-218); vol. 9, p. 15 (K1-215; K1-216); vol 16, p. 39 (K1-3884).

25. **Ayliffe**, p. 33.

26. [I have failed to trace the detailed account which seems to lie behind this opening section. The trade token is noted and illustrated in W. G. St. L. Finny, *The Royal Borough of Kingston upon Thames,* (1902), p. 144 (no. 16).]

27 Progress here owes much to the vigilence and initiative of J. Sampson. The present owner, Mr. A. W. E. Valler, kindly supplied her with copies of the documents. I am very grateful to both.

28. The architectural summary is based on information supplied by Mr. I. J. .West.

29. **PRO** E179/188/481; 179/188/496.

30. **KPR(Bu)** 26th. March 1674.

31. **KBR** KF1/1/25.

32. 'Pearson' is the most common form in this source. Other forms include Pearsone, Peerson, Peirson, Perceson, Person, Perseson and Pierson.

33. **Apprentices**, nos. 521, 538, 742, 806, 823 and 873.

34. **KPR(B)** 16th. February 1611/12; **KPR(Bu)** 29th. September 1673.

35. **KPR(B)** 1st. November 1635; **KPR(Bu)** 12th. March 1724/25.

36. **KPR(B)** 16th. August 1660; **KPR(Bu)** 12th. March 1724/5.

37. **KBR** KE2/5/1.

38. **Apprentices**, no. 1407.

39. [For other local examples, see below, Papers XI and XII.]

40. [The postscript first appeared as a separate item in **KUTAS NL** 5 (March 1980).]

41. **BPR(Bu)** 5th. May 1695 and 30th. January 1695/96.

42. For background see F. W. Steer, *Farm and Cottage Inventories of Mid-Essex, 1635-1749,* (1969).

43. **KBR** KF4/1/10-13, 29.

44. **Sampson**, pp. 72-73, 87; **KBR** KB42/1; 42/2.

45. **KBR** KC4/3/2-3.

46. **KBR** KE2/5/1.

47. Published 1731 (copy in BL).

48. **KBR** KB9/1, p. 260.

49. [For the Gallows, see above, Paper VII.]

50. **KBR** KB9/1; 9/2.

51. *Kelly's Kingston Directory,* (1894). For a sketch of the building in 1838 see the collection mentioned under n. 1, above, (also printed in **SC** 21st. June 1985). Other early pictures are in **KHC** file prints.

XI

155-157 LONDON ROAD

[Miss Wakeford shared with her K.U.T.A.S. colleagues deep concern about the destructive impact of modern redevelopment on Kingston's architectural heritage, and she expressed this concern in practical ways, most notably by representing K.U.T.A.S. on the Kingston Old Town Conservation Area Advisory Committee (from c. 1980 onwards) and by joining others in campaigning for the preservation of buildings under threat. In the latter context her particular contribution took the form of detailed research into the histories of endangered buildings, and the presentation of her findings in written form, as part of larger reports prepared for submission to public enquiries. The most successful campaign to which she contributed was in 1971. This resulted in the preservation of Picton House and the subsequent publication of Picton House and the People Connected with it, (KUTAS Occasional Paper No. 2, 1979). The present paper, written in partnership with Mr. I. J, West in 1977, was drafted as part of a campaign to save Nos. 155/157 London Road, a Grade 2 listed building, threatened by London Transport redevelopment proposals. In this case local efforts were in vain, and the site is now occupied by London Transport's 'bus depot.]

At the time of destruction Nos. 155/157 London Road were a pair of semi-detached houses with a Gothic facade and, at roof level, a suggestion of castellation which in recent years had earned the building the name 'Snapper's Castle' (after the proprietor of the shop at No. 157) {1}. It had been a gentleman's house, a school and the parish workhouse, and assumed its final form in 1841/2. The houses were thereafter called Manor House and Manor House West, in the belief that the old house had been the manor house of the lost manor of *Hertingtoncombe*. It has proved impossible to find any authority for this theory, which seems to be based on a suggestion of Manning and Bray {2}. Their idea arose directly from their mistaken identification of the house with Hercombe Place, which was in Heathen (now Eden) Street {3}. Biden drew attention to this error as long ago as 1852, but it has nevertheless been repeated in later works {4}. No documentary reference to the house as Hertington Manor House has been found. The site belonged to Kingston Manor, to which its owners paid two quit-rents of 1s. each, and in the rolls of which it is described simply as a messuage and land in Norbiton {5}. It is proposed here to refer to the old house as 'the mansion house' and to the later semi-detached houses as Nos. 155/157 London Road. It is sometimes said that the mansion house had been physically moved down from Richmond Park: this seems to be a modern story, probably arising from the association with Hertingdon, which was enclosed in the Park in 1637.

The Builder

Nos. 155/157 were built by Charles Molloy Westmacott soon after 1840, when he is shown in the Kingston Tithe Apportionment as owning 3 roods 15 perches of land, with the old workhouse buildings and gardens {6}. In the 1841 Census the two houses are shown as in course of construction, and in Brayley's county history of 1843, Mr. Westmacott's 'pretty cottages' are mentioned {7}. A cottage at that time was a country residence in a romantic style, rather than the humble dwelling the word would now signify, and the houses were occupied by professional people for many years. They were a rare Kingston survivor of the early nineteenth century Gothic style, a modest example of the exuberant Victorian habit of adapting a variety of historical features to make a building characteristic of no century but its own. The architect is not known, but may well have been Westmacott himself, or some connection of his.

Charles Molloy Westmacott belonged to a large and well-known family of sculptors, artists and architects. According to one authority, he was the illegitimate son of Sir Richard Westmacott R.A. (1775-1856): his mother was Susan Molloy, a widow who was the landlady of The Bull and Horns at Fulham {8}. As Charles was between 46 and 50 in 1841, his father's indiscretion must have been an early one and the son was evidently acknowledged and supported by him: he was educated at Eton and Oxford and is referred to as a sculptor (he exhibited a bust of the actor J. P. Kemble at the Royal Academy in 1822). Sir Richard was a well-known sculptor who was constantly in demand for large national monuments for St. Paul's, Westminster Abbey or open spaces in London and other cities. The colossal bronze statue of Achilles in Hyde Park and the Duke of York on his column in Waterloo Place are his, and he was partly responsible for the reliefs on Marble Arch and the pediment of the portico of the British Museum. Charles M. Westmacott described himself to the 1841 Census enumerator as a printer, by which he probably meant publisher {9}. He was an art critic and art historian and the editor of various periodicals, best-known for *The Age* and *Records of the Arts*. Writing sometimes under the pseudonym Bernard Blackmantle (and perhaps even Abel Funnefello!), he was the author of several humorous works, including *The Punster's Pocket Book*, 'a two-act musical farce' and *The English Spy*, 'an original work, characteristic, satirical and humorous, comprising scenes and sketches in every rank of society, being portraits of the illustrious, eminent, eccentric and notorious'. He even tried his hand at a two-volume novel, *Fitzalleyne of Berkley*, 'a romance of the present times'.

To design a Gothic house might seem a fairly likely undertaking for such a man, and the fact that the internal arrangments of the two houses bear an imperfect relationship to the exterior (in particular the outer ground-floor windows are blocked by the stairways) could be explained by his not being a professional architect. However, the facade of Nos. 155/157 London Road is described by a recent authority as 'Tudor Gothic', and the term suggests that the building might also be the work of the architect William Westmacott (apparently the son, or possibly the younger brother, of Sir Richard), who was designing cottages from 1816 to 1848 and whose St. Mark's Hall in Long Acre is referred to elsewhere as 'Jacobethan'{10}. The corner turrets and

XXXI. Nos. 155/157 London Road, alias 'Snappers Castle', 1956. The threat of destruction in 1971 occasioned a vigorous, but ultimately unsuccessful campaign for their preservation. (**KHC** file print K1-1302).

XXXII. Norbiton Place, the home of Charles N. Pallmer MP. It was the sale of the substantial estate attached to this house in 1836 which made possible C. M. Westmacott's association with the area. (**KHC** file print K1-189).

'Gothic Labels' over the lower windows of Nos. 155/157 London Road may owe something to the 'Castellated Gothic' cottages of Loudon's *Encyclopaedia of Cottage, Farm and Villa Architecture and Furniture*, published only a few years earlier and widely used as a pattern-book, but the Kingston design as a whole is considerably more restrained and perhaps still under some eighteenth-century influence.

C. M. Westmacott is not known to have occupied either of the houses himself, but he was living in Kingston in the 1830s and 1840s. Ayliffe, purporting to describe the town in 1837, says he lived in the large old house, said to have been built by Vanbrugh, which stood on the corner of the narrow alley beside the Lovekyn Chapel {11}. Records of this period are scanty and contain no indication that Mr. Westmacott lived in this house, but Massey Dawson, who had occupied it for many years, had died about 1830 and Mr. Westmacott may well have been a tenant for a while. In 1836, the large Norbiton Place estate built up by Charles N. Pallmer, came on the market. Details of the purchasers have not been found, but according to the 1840 Tithe Map, C. M. Westmacott then owned a small piece of land (1r. 24p.), with house, garden and buildings, in the corner between the present London and Coombe Roads {12}. He also had a cottage further along Coombe Road, and according to a note on a plan of part of the Norbiton Place estate prepared for the auction of the house itself and its pleasure grounds, he had also proposed to buy about 20 acres of meadow adjoining the present Cambridge Road, but for some reason had withdrawn from that purchase {13}. He already had the London Road land by 1838, and a villa and lodge had by then been built on it {14}. It was then occupied by Charles Heath, who had bought at the auction a big area of parkland and ornamental water adjoining the house on the Coombe Road side. It is thus not clear who was the original purchaser of the small house site, but it seems likely that C. M. Westmacott had the house built and he was living there by 1840. In the 1841 Census, it is called "Kingston Lodge" (the quotation marks are in the Enumerator's Book) and the mutilated remains of it still have that name {15}. Now only the castellated roof-line of its miniature keep can be seen above the huddle of small buildings around it. The tiny lodge facing London Road (demolished in 1927) apparently had small corner turrets like those on Nos. 155/157 London Road {16}. Whether or not C. M. Westmacott was the designer of both Kingston Lodge and Nos. 155/157 London Road, they show the direction of his tastes, though the former house seems to have been more elaborate and pretentious, as perhaps befits one intended for his own occupation. The 1841 Census books are less informative than those of later years, and the relationship to C. M. Westmacott of the other residents of Kingston Lodge (Charles William F. Westmacott, aged 12 and Anne Westmacott, aged 35, in that order) is not clear. There was also one servant 'living in', a very modest household for the period and the district. Mr. Westmacott no longer lived at Kingston Lodge by the 1851 Census and may have died in the late 1840s: his will has not yet been traced.

The Building

As to Nos. 155/157 London Road, it is clear that the facade, the interior and the oriel windows in the side walls belonged entirely to the rebuilding of

1841. Older panelling had been re-used to make the corner front-room over the stairs in both houses. It is said that some of the panelling came from Kensington Palace, and it may have been acquired by C. M. Westmacott, whose grandfather Richard Westmacott the elder (1747-1808) was appointed Mason for the Palace in 1796, and evidently passed on his contacts there to his sons Richard and Henry, both of whom received large payments for work there in 1807-10, mainly for elaborate marble chimney pieces {18}. There was an interesting three-part carved panel in the door of the cupboard under the stairs in the hall of No. 155; the top part had turned balusters, the centre a female figure holding a cross in her right hand and surrounded by inter-twined flowers and fruit, the bottom part a similar figure, but holding a bird.

The ground floor of each house had two main rooms divided by sliding doors (those in No. 157 having been removed before demolition). These doors, the entrance doors of both houses and the door of a cupboard in the front room of No. 155 were of oak with four lancet-headed panels with quadrangular insets at about one-third of the height. This work presumably dated from 1841. The stairs had graceful turned balusters. The window of the first floor back room of No. 155 had slender folding shutters with carved cover-boards, and in this house there was carving between the door and window in the conservatory. The corresponding windows in No. 157 seemed to have copper settings. No. 155 also had a fine moulded stone surround to the kitchen fireplace. Although the two conservatories were of the same period, their doors and windows, which had similar mouldings, had different proportions, perhaps an indication that whatever was available at the time had been used. The air-bricks at the rear (in the walls of the W.C.s and of the extension to No. 155) were of decorated terra cotta and over the back doors and those of the W.C.s were moulded scroll supports with flat stone heads. We were told of a 'tunnel' said to run from the cupboard in the south-east corner of the front room in No. 155 to the opposite corner of the house and under a large shed in the back garden: presumably this was a sewer, rather than the 'secret passage' of modern fantasy.

Nairn and Pevsner noticed the side door of No. 157, which had a straight hood on carved brackets, and dated the building as late-seventeenth-century (apart of course from the facade) {19}. The side and back walls were of dark red bricks laid in random bond, quite uncharacteristic of nineteenth century work, (even if it had been intended that the whole should be stuccoed like the front). It seems likely that, following the common practice in Kingston in the past, the 1841 builders retained what they could of the old house. This is confirmed by Ayliffe who refers to the parish workhouse 'most of which was pulled down in 1837, but part of the building was turned into two dwelling-houses which still stand immediately opposite the end of Coombe Lane' {20}. The workhouse image had to be lost and this was achieved by the new facade and such picturesque details as the oriel windows at the side, the corner turrets and the four tall 'ecclesiastical' windows at first floor level (the bay window of No. 157 was evidently a later alteration). Comparison of Hornor's 1813 map of Kingston, the Tithe map of 1840 and the 25-inch Ordnance Survey map of 1863 indicates that Nos. 155/157 were on the same alignment and site as, and much the same size as, the main body of the old building, though the outbuildings were demolished.

Assuming that part of the previous house had survived, it must have been a seventeenth-century building. A drawing of 1837 is in the Heritage Centre and is reproduced in Merryweather's local history as 'The Old Workhouse'. It shows curved Dutch gables and a cluster of very tall, presumably brick, chimneys. That the bricks of the old walls are not laid in English bond is not significant, for in the early seventeenth century the brick trades were only beginning to be established here (stimulated by the royal works in brick in the sixteenth century, notably Hampton Court). In fact regular bonding has not been found in Kingston for the seventeenth century, either in the few buildings surviving into our own time (in particular Cleave's Almshouses of 1670, the slightly earlier No. 30 London Road, and the mid-century Coombe Hill Farmhouse, all in random bond) or in the datable brickwork revealed in excavations (in Vicarage Road or on the Bishops Hall site or on the wharf by the Old Bridge, where the house was built in accordance with covenants in a lease of 1697) {21}.

Brick gables very similar to those shown in the 1837 drawing survive in a few Surrey houses which can be fairly securely dated to the earlier part of the seventeenth century. The Old Manor House in Old Woking High Street has a western gable with an identical silhouette, with the bricks laid in an irregular English bond. This was probably built (round a sixteenth-century, smoke-bay house) by Sir Edward Zouch about 1630, after James I had granted him the Woking Manor and he had demolished the old palace there {22}. There is a similar gable in Millstream House (formerly Old House, and previously the Mill House) at Shalford: it is interesting that Shalford, like Kingston, had a medieval Tile-house, and by the end of the sixteenth century several families working as brickmakers and bricklayers {23}. Ripley Manor has a similar gable {24}. Bricks were commonly used for domestic building earlier in the eastern counties than elsewhere and an early seventeenth century view of the Tuesday Market Place at King's Lynn shows gables of this shape {25}. Nairn and Pevsner refer to the various Surrey buildings with Dutch gables as being in the 'Artisan Style' and seem to relate most of them to the early or middle seventeenth century {26}. Presumably the style spread with the craft of building in brick from East Anglia in the late sixteenth century.

Historical Associations

The old mansion house may be attributed to the early seventeenth century not only on ground of style but also on the evidence of the earliest printed reference yet found to the building (apart from Lovibond's poem quoted later)., A letter written in 1798 by J.P. Malcolm (who had visited Kingston while engraving local views for Lysons) says, 'At the entrance of Kingston from London stands the workhouse, formerly a school; the date on a spout 1629' (a drainpipe with a large head is conspicuous in the 1837 drawing) {27}. It happens that the neighbouring Norbiton Hall was described in 1631 as 'new built in brick' {28}. Mr. Robert Harrison there shown as paying the Grammar School quit-rent for the Hall, was presumably related to the Wood family (Roger Wood of Islington, Serjeant at Arms, who died seised of Norbiton Hall in 1623, married a Miss Harrison), and he may have been a trustee of the infant heir, Robert Wood {29}. By the time of the Surrey Hearth Tax Assessment of 1664, both houses were owned by the Wood family (the mansion house was assessed at 15 hearths and was empty) {30}. It is possible therefore that both were built or rebuilt in brick at the same time for that family. Of Sir Robert Wood, it was stated in 1644 that he was one of the Committee for Safety for Surrey in the Civil War, 'and has been plundered of his estate of Kingston by the King's force and has a fort built on his land at Islington' {31}.

The Rous Period

The next reference to the mansion house is in the Surrey Hearth Tax of 1674, when John Rous was assessed there for 15 hearths. Both the number of hearths (Norbiton Hall had 13 and Norbiton Place 23) and the status of the Rous family indicate that the mansion house was a gentleman's residence of a fair size {32}. John Rous had been born in Barbados and his father, a wealthy owner of sugar plantations, had promised a settlement of £ 20,000 on the son's marriage (probably later reduced, owing to the father's remarriage, to £ 10,000, still a large sum at the time) {33}. John Rous had thrown in his lot with the Quakers as early as 1656 and suffered in the cause by being imprisoned, whipped and sentenced to have an ear cut off by the authorities in New England. In 1662 he married Margaret Fell junior, daughter of Judge Thomas Fell and of that Margaret Fell who in 1669 married George Fox. John and Margaret Rous at first lived at Mile End Green but in a letter of 4th. November 1670 to his wife's sister, Sarah Fell, he wrote 'We are now pretty well settled in our house at Kingston' {34}. Rous is said to have built 'a handsome house at Kingston, Surrey, converted later into a workhouse', but the authority for this is uncertain {35}. It may be derived from a late-nineteenth-century study of the Fell family, where it is said of the house mentioned in Rous's will '(it) had been erected by himself. It was an Elizabethan (*sic*) building and stood till lately in an elevated suburb of Kingston called Surbiton (*sic*). It was ultimately purchased for a parish workhouse; but its site is now graced by some fashionable villas' {36}. Here, again, no authority is given, nor has any been found in the manuscript material in the Friends' Library. In view of the evidence that John Rous's house existed in 1664 with the same number of hearths as when he had it in 1674, as well as the 1629 date, it seems likely that some reference to his 'new house', meaning a house to which he had lately moved, has been misinterpreted.

The Rous family had eight or nine children, only four of whom survived infancy. During their 25 years at the mansion house not only Mrs. Fox and her daughters, but also George Fox himself often stayed with them. Fox used it as a base for many of his journeys and would go there for peace for his writing. He was also called on for moral support and comfort when there was illness in the family. He recounts in his *Journal* that when staying there in 1673 'I had a vision when I was lying in my bed at Kingston; I saw that I was taken prisoner and I saw also that I rid down into a deep steep water three times and up again'; soon afterwards he was taken to Worcester Gaol {37}.

John Rous carried on business from London as a West India merchant. He played a considerable part in the affairs of the Kingston Meeting of the Quakers, particularly in business matters, such as the acquisition of a site for a meeting house and in keeping the books of the Meeting. His letters to Margaret Fox were often concerned with legal and financial subjects and he was evidently one of those Friends who early set the movement on the path of orderliness in practical matters and moderation and common sense in personal relationships for which it has since been noted. He returned several times to Barbados in connection with both his family and business interests and the organisation of the Friends there. His father's standing in the island and his acquaintance with the Governor were a great help to the movement and in the early days large meetings were held on his plantation {38}. Late in 1693, John Rous went again to Barbados and this time he did not return, for his ship was lost on the way back in 1695. By his will he left the house to his widow for life during widowhood, with 'reasonable use' of its contents. His son Nathaniel, who was entitled to the greater part of the estate, married soon after his father's death. The widow sold the house to Edward Belitha {39}.

Archbishop Tillotson

Before passing on to the Belitha period, it is necessary to consider the statement, apparently first made by Brayley, that the mansion house had once been occupied by 'Archbishop Tillotson' {40}. John Tillotson (1630-94) was, according to MaCaulay, the most popular preacher of his time. He was Archbishop of Canterbury during only the last three years of his life; immediately before that he had been Dean of St. Paul's. His early connections appear to have been with the Puritans, but later his talents were employed in weaning men from Puritan ideas {41}. Eighteenth-century biographies do not mention that he ever lived in Kingston, and he does not appear in the few surviving local assessments of the time {42}. He had a house at Edmonton, as well as the Deanery of St. Paul's and, later, apartments at Lambeth Palace. On the other hand, John Rous several times went to Barbados and his wife either went with him or went to stay in London. There is a tax assessment for 1680 in which the house does not appear, but by the next surviving assessment for 1683, Rous is again taxed there {43}. It is quite possible that the house was let to Dr. Tillotson during the absence of the Rous family, at this or some other time. He preached the Assize sermon at Kingston on 21st. July 1681 on 'The Lawfulness and Obligation of Oaths', a big issue of the day, 'some making conscience of taking any oaths at all, and too many none at all of breaking them' {44}. The Quakers of course refused to take oaths. The Archbishop's very last sermon was also preached at Kingston, on 29th. July 1694, but on 28th. June 1694 he was writing from Lambeth, where he died in the following November, so it does not seem likely that he lived at Kingston at that time {45}. Whether or not Dr. Tillotson used the house from time to time, modern references to it as 'once an archbishop's palace' are hardly justified.

Edward Belitha

Edward Belitha Esq., who bought the house from Margaret Rous in 1696 was a citizen of London and presumably a business man. As far as is known he occupied the house himself for the rest of his life and he certainly took an interest in local affairs. One of the burning topics of the day in Kingston (perhaps a consequence of the more settled times and greater prosperity of the early eighteenth century) was the question of education and of the proper use of existing endowments for the purpose. The Grammar School, which taught young gentlemen or would-be professional men, mainly Latin and Greek, was of little benefit to most Kingston people, whose children would have to earn a living in trade or as artisans. The Tiffin charity established in the seventeenth century had provided for 'honest poor men's sons' of Kingston to be taught to write and cast accounts and to be apprenticed to a trade, and the smaller Brown's charity had much the same objects but was not restricted to boys {46}. One result of the public discussion which evidently took place in the first decade of the eighteenth century was the will dated 1710 of Nicholas Hardinge, providing an endowment with the same objects as Tiffin's, but for poor boys and girls {47}. At the same time Edward Belitha paid a woman to teach girls, and when he died in 1717 he left £ 400, the interest on which was to be used to employ 'some honest reputable woman . . . . to teach twenty poor persons' daughters of the said town to read and work plain work well', in the first instance using the same teacher as he had already employed {48}. The phrase 'work plain work well' has lost its significance in the age of sewing machines and mass-production, but it indicated that these working-class girls were to be taught working-class sewing, making endless seams, hemming, patching and darning, not the fine embroidery which the children of gentlefolk learned. The ability to read and do plain sewing would fit them to earn their living and to be good wives as well, and during a century and a half many Kingston girls must have had reason to be grateful to Mr. Belitha for the opportunity to improve their lot.

Edward Belitha died in 1717 in his 76th. year and was buried in the church of St. Dunstan in the East in London, where a marble tablet was placed in memory of him. His only son William was, like him, public-spirited and charitable. He became High Sheriff of Surrey in 1720 and he was also associated with Dr. Thomas Bray's foundation of about 1724 for converting the negroes on British plantations in America. This led on to an interest in Georgia and he was one of the nine original members of the Common Council of the Georgia Trust. He resigned fairly soon owing to ill-health, but remained a trustee and helped by collecting and donating funds to the Trust. He was also an early member of the Society for the Propagation of the Gospel {49}. William Belitha sold the mansion house to Nicholas Hardinge in 1736 and apparently moved to Teddington.

The Grammar School Period

Nicholas Hardinge, who bought the house in 1738, was a celebrated lawyer, classical scholar and antiquary, Chief Clerk to the House of Commons and a most notable Recorder of Kingston. In 1737 he inherited from his cousin, also Nicholas Hardinge, the manor of Kingston Canbury and on 19th. December 1738, he married the daughter of the Lord Chief Justice of England. As part of the financial arrangements following on these events, Nicholas Hardinge on 17/18th. December 1738 mortgaged some of his properties, including the

64

house he had bought from William Belitha {50}. The house is described in these deeds as 'all that capital messuage or mansion house called New Brickhouse in Norbiton', and there were also eleven acres of land in four closes behind or near the messuage and adjoining one another, and a further two acres used as an orchard, near the messuage but lying between London Lane and Martins Lane (i.e. Coombe Lane - so the orchard must have been on the other side of the road, opposite the house). The eleven acres and two acres were later disposed of separately from the house and its garden, etc., probably for the market gardens which are known later to have surrounded it.

The phrase 'called New Brickhouse' in the 1738 deeds must not be thought to indicate that the mansion house had only recently been built: rather the contrary, for in the case of a house built in Kingston in the 1730s it would be taken for granted that it was in brick and the fact would not be mentioned. Much earlier, when brick building was novel, it was customary to use this phrase (decidedly archaic in form by 1738), as in the 1631 reference noted earlier {51}. Once it was in the title deeds, it would be copied from one document to another for generations; when the mansion house was conveyed to the Parish of Kingston in 1774, the same words were used {52}.

The next phase in the history of the mansion house is interesting for quite different reasons, Nicholas Hardinge had a large house in Canbury and had evidently not bought William Belitha's house for his own use. It may be that he had not bought it as a profitable investment either, for it was now to be occupied for 35 years by Mr. Richard Wooddeson, M.A., who had been appointed master of the Free Grammar School in Kingston on 1st. February 1732 {53}. Mr. Wooddeson had a considerable reputation as a school master and during his period the Grammar School flourished. The master's salary of £ 30 *per annum* was by this time inadequate, even though the repairs to the premises (i.e. the Lovekyn Chapel and the master's house) were met from the income of the endowment and the school had the use of the field opposite as a playing-field. Like many other endowed grammar schools at this period, the alternatives were to let the school wither away or to allow the master to take private fee-paying pupils and this practice was already established in Kingston at least as early as 1708, when the master complained to the bailiffs that John Smith's son had 'beat some of the young gentlemen boarders at the school' {54}. According to Biden, 'The School obtained considerable celebrity about a hundred years ago, under the able management of Mr. Wooddeson, who was obliged to hire another house in consequence of the large number of scholars placed under his instruction. The scholars under Mr. Wooddeson's care varied in number from 80 to 100 and consisted of members of aristocratic families alone, who not only claimed none of the privileges of the School as a Free Endowed School, but in the only case in which those privileges were claimed, so maltreated the unfortunate youth whose father had the temerity to seek those advantages, that he was *mercifully* removed, and thus the intentions of the Royal Founder were for the time entirely frustrated' {55}. Biden, writing in 1852, was not quite right about the pupils, for it is clear that many of them were not aristocrats, but were rather from the gentry, professional classes and wealthy merchants living in the fashionable Twickenham and Teddington, as well as in Kingston itself, Hampton, Putney and Richmond. A former pupil, Gilbert Wakefield

(1756-1801), a religious and political controversialist of some note and the son of the then vicar of Kingston wrote that Mr. Wooddeson continued at Kingston until 1772 'with signal success and equal reputation. A considerable portion of the nobility and gentry in that neighbourhood, who had been educated within the period here specified, were trained under him' {56}. It seems indeed that the history of the Grammar School at this period anticipated by a century that of those old endowed grammar schools which, under pressure from, and with the financial support of the upper middle classes, were revived as exclusive boarding schools and are now known as Public Schools. Nicholas Hardinge sent his own eldest son, George (later a judge, a friend of Horace Walpole and the original of 'the waggish Welsh judge Jefferies Hardsman' in Byron's 'Don Juan') to the school: it may be that he had understood the need for this type of school and had bought the mansion specifically to help Mr. Wooddeson to expand. (Wooddeson evidently had no private means and according to Gilbert Wakefield left his widow unprovided for).

Gilbert Wakefield who had a poor opinion of other schoolmasters under whom he had suffered, said of Wooddeson 'on this gentleman I never reflect but with sensations of pleasure and sentiments of respect. He was indeed, generally beloved by all his scholars' {57}. A very pleasant impression of life at the school at this time is given in the poems of another former pupil, Edward Lovibond of Hampton, some lines from which are given in an appendix to these notes. It is unfortunate that Mr. Wooddeson's most famous pupil, the historian Edward Gibbon, author of *The Decline and Fall of the Roman Empire,* should have recorded his less happy memories, saying 'in my ninth year (i.e. January 1746) in a lucid interval of comparative health, my father adopted the convenient and customary mode of English education; and I was sent to Kingston upon Thames to a school of about seventy boys, which was kept by Mr. Wooddeson and his assistants. Want of strength and activity disqualified me for the sports of the playfield, nor have I forgotten how often in the year 1746 I was reviled and buffeted for the sins of my Tory ancestors. By the common methods of discipline, at the expense of many tears and some blood, I purchased the knowledge of the Latin syntax; and not long since I was possessed of the dirty volumes of Phaedras and Cornelius Nepos, which I painfully construed and darkly understood. My studies were too frequently interrupted by sickness, and after a real or nominal residence at Kingston School of near two years, I was finally recalled' {58}. The fact that his father, like other High Tories of the time, was thought to be a Jacobite would not make the boy popular in the year after the '45 rebellion.

Greek and Latin made up the greater part of the curriculum of the grammar schools, but Dr. Wooddeson, who is said by Gilbert Wakefield not to have been a great classical scholar, 'was very rigid in requiring elegant English from his scholars in construing Greek and Latin authors, almost to a degree of fastidious affectation' {59}. The result was a crop of writers of excellent English prose and poetry, many of whom achieved the posthumous glory of an entry in the *Dictionary of National Biography.* Besides those already mentioned, there were the poet and critic William Hayley, who nearly lost his life when an epidemic struck the school because Mrs. Wooddeson 'had a dangerous propensity to dabble in medicine and thought herself perfectly able, with the aid of an ignorant apothecary, to manage the most

66

Vera
Effigies
GUILIELMI BVRTON
LL. Bacca. *Laurei.*

XXXIV. A contemporary engraving of William Burton, one of Mr. Richard Wooddeson's distinguished predecessors as Master of Kingston Grammar School. A classical scholar of some repute, his works included a commentary on the Antonine Itinerary (see page 2). (**BL** CRACH.1.Tabl.b.1, vol. IV, following p. 358).

XXXIII. An anonymous portrait of Archbishop Tillotson, who may have resided briefly in the house which became Nos. 155/157 London Road towards the end of the seventeenth century. (**KHC** file print K1-387).

XXXV. London Road in 1931, with the metal lines of the town's tram service in the foreground and Norbiton Hall at the rear. The camera is positioned approximately at the junction of London Road and Coombe Road. (**KHC** file print K1-3621).

XXXVI. Norbiton Hall, c. 1921. The site of the house is now occupied by the large block of brick-built flats at the junction of London Road and Birkenhead Avenue. (**KHC** file print K1-3619).

formidable disorders', {60}; George Stevens, a Shakespearian editor; George Keate of Isleworth, writer, naturalist, antiquary and artist, and a friend of Voltaire; Francis Maseres, mathematician and historian, the first holder of the Chancellor's Medal at Cambridge; and Wooddeson's own son, also Richard, Vinerian Professor of English Law, who is said to have made 'an important contribution towards systematisation of English law' {61}.

Owing to age and infirmity, Mr. Wooddeson retired in 1772 and went to live in Chelsea. He died in 1774. His successor as Grammar School master did not continue with the mansion and it was put on the market. It happened that Kingston Vestry, then responsible for poor relief, was looking for a new workhouse, for the house in Surbiton Lane, on the corner of the later Woodbines estate, which had been used since 1725, was probably even older. In 1774, the former Grammar School mansion was bought by Kingston Parish for £650, for conversion into a workhouse. The purchase money was advanced by twenty leading inhabitants of Kingston, who were to be repaid within three years out of the Poor Rate and meanwhile had a charge on the house {62}. Edward Lovibond's poem 'On the converting the late Mr, Wooddeson's house at Kingston into a Poor-house and cutting down the great walk of high trees before it' points to a feature of the site which may have unsuspected implications {63}. Lovibond was inspired by nostalgia and by regret at the loss of the trees; we may wonder why the trees were planted there, for they were not on land belonging to the mansion and had not been intended as an amenity for its occupants. When Edward Belitha bought the mansion house from Margaret Rous in 1696, he entered into a separate transaction with Kingston Corporation as lords of the manor of Kingston. By a deed dated 25th. June 1696 he paid £14 to have for 99 years the fourteen ash and elm trees standing on the manorial waste before his house (not the ground on which they stood), with power to him to cut down any of them, but in that case he was to replace them {64}. The Rocque map of 1745 clearly shows the row of trees (in fact 13 of them) and they stand immediately opposite the end of Coombe Road, formerly Coombe Lane or Merton Lane. Biden says that the road from London was a continuation of this road and that it passed originally at the *back* of Norbiton Hall. Presumably he refers to local tradition, but certainly the present London Road was originally a mere lane (it is referred to in Canbury manor documents as *venella*) {65}. The old road was evidently the medieval way from Merton Priory to its manor of Kingston Canbury, but it may well antedate the manor, given to Merton early in the twelfth century. It may be that when the trade centre of Kingston had become established upstream from the earlier focal point, the Corporation deliberately diverted the London entry to the two through Norbiton, planted a row of trees at this point to close the way through Canbury and granted the mansion site (by a document not yet traced) for a rental of 1s.

The Workhouse Period

The mansion house remained the parish workhouse for over 60 years. Even after the Poor Law Amendment Act of 1834, under which the parish became one of 13 parishes making up the Kingston Union, the new Guardians, having by the end of 1836 closed the workhouses of all other parishes, intended to use the former mansion house as a central workhouse for the whole Union and they did so until September 1839, paying a rent to the parish for it. According to a printed report of a committee set up by the Kingston Vestry in 1835 to examine the state of the Workhouse (in connection with problems which had arisen while it served the parish only), there were then 63 inmates {66}. When the Union was working it was realised that the Guardians would have to provide for about 250. A committee which they set up reported at the beginning of 1827 that 'the Committee has never been insensible of the very imperfect nature of the accommodation of the Kingston house after making all the improvements which were attainable without a material alteration of the structure of the premises' {67}. The Committee concluded 'while the situation upon a great public road in the immediate vicinity of a large town, on a low plain and with an area of inconvenient shape and under 2 acres in extent, present so many objections to incurring any considerable expenditure upon this scite as to make it more eligible in the opinion of this committee at once to choose for a permanent establishment a new scite in a higher and more detached situation, where a Workhouse and premises of the most eligible plan may be built'. When the decision to buy the new site was endorsed by the poor Law Commissioners, a parish meeting of 31st. October 1839 resolved 'that the said property should be sold by public auction in one lot'. The property was described as freehold and consisting of 'an old mansion house with outbuildings and about one acre and a half of land' (later found to be only about one acre) and it was stated that the premises 'are much out of repair and could not be turned to good account without considerable outlay'. A Sale Order was issued by the Commissioners on 12th. December 1839, the sale was advertised fifteen times and the property was sold by auction on 9th. January 1840 to C.M. Westmacott for £1050. Completion did not take place until the end of May 1840, partly because Mr. Westmacott wished to apply to the Corporation for the grant of a strip of land in front of the premises. Although there are no plans or descriptions of the building among the documents relating to sale and the preceding decisions of the Committee, it is clear that the mansion was neither demolished nor structurally altered before the sale to Mr. Westmacott.

Appendix

Some lines concerning the mansion house and life at Mr. Wooddeson's school, from *Poems on Several Occasions* by Edward Lovibond, published postumously 1787.

On the converting the late Mr. Wooddeson's House at Kingston into a Poor-house, and cutting down the great walk of high trees before it. (extracts)

> Where the broad pathway fronts yon ancient seat,
> Approach not, stranger, with unhallow'd feet,
> Nor mock the spot, unshelter'd now, and bare !
> The grove's old honours rose majestic there,
> Its giant arms extending to defend
> Thy revered temples, man's and Virtue's friend !

Secure thy walk that unpierc'd gloom along,
No storm approach'd to silence Homer's song;
No beam to wound thy Heaven-directed eye;
The world's near tumult swept unheeded by.
Now, low as thine, these towering heads are laid,
Nor more embower the mansion in their shade,
Time-honour'd pile ! that, owning thee its lord,
Saw ancient manners, ancient faith, restor'd;
In renovated youth beheld again
Saturnian days, the good Eliza's reign,
With thee too sheltering many an angel quest,
For what, but Heaven, serener than thy breast ?
Blest mansion then, Simplicity's abode,
Where smiling Innocence look'd up to God,
Where Nature's genuine graces charm'd the heart,
Or Nature, polish'd but by classic art.
There Fancy, warm'd with brightest, chastest beams,
The saint's high rapture, and the poet's dreams,
While Virtue left, delighting there to dwell,
The pensive mountain and the hermit's cell.
There the good teacher held by turns to youth
The blaze of fiction and pure light of truth,
Who, less by precept than example fir'd,
Glow'd as he taught, inspiring and inspir'd.
Nor think, gay revellers, this awful roof
Echoed no sound but Wisdom's harsh reproof;
The social board, attendant Mirth, was there,
The smile unconscious of tomorrow's care,
With every tranquil joy of wedded life,
The gracious children, and the faithful wife.
. . . . .
While yet this humbler pile survives to prove
A mansion worthy of the master's love.
Like him, still welcomes to its liberal door
Whom most he honour'd, honouring most the poor;
Like him, the lisping infant's blessing shares,
And Age's gratitude in silent prayers.
While such partake the couch, the frugal feast,
No regal chambers boast an equal guest;
For, gracious Maker, by thy own decree,
Receiving mercy is receiving Thee !

1. I am grateful for the help of the Kingston Assistant Borough Archivist and of the staffs of the Surrey Record Office and Kingston Heritage Centre.

2. **M&B**, vol I, p. 404.

3. [See above, Paper VI.]

4. **Biden**, p.99, note 'j', also pp. 23-24. The error is perpetuated, e.g. in **VCH Surrey**, vol III, p. 503.

5. **KBR** KF1/1.

6. **SRO** P33/2/1 (plot 1564).

7. **Brayley**, vol III, p. 46.; 1841 Census (microfilm in **KHC**).

8. R. Gunnis, *Dictionary of British Sculptors 1660-1851*, article *Westmacott, Sir Richard R.A.* The following paragraph draws heavily on this account.

9. 1841 Census (microfilm in **KHC**).

10. H. R. Hitchcock, *Early Victorian Architecture in Britain*, 2nd. ed., (1972), p. 333.

11. **Ayliffe**, p. 15.

12. **SRO** P33/2/1 (plot 365).

13. **SRO** 266/4/105. I am grateful to the Kingston Assistant Borough Archivist for drawing my attention to this reference.

14. **SRO** 635.

15. 1841 Census (microfilm in **KHC**).

16. **SC** 31st. August 1974 (article by J. Sampson on George Meredith).

17. 1851 Census (microfilm in **KHC**).

18. R. Gunnis, *op. cit.* (above, n. 8). The following section on the architectural history of the building is the contribution of Mr. I. J. West.

19. **Pevsner,Surrey**, p. 335.

20. **Ayliffe**, p. 15.

21. **Merryweather**, p.25; **KBR** KC1/1/118.

22. According to **DBRG(S).**

23. R. Nevill, *Old Cottage and Domestic Architecture in South-west Surrey*, (1891), p. 96: **PNSurrey**, p. 247.

24. **Pevsner,Surrey**, p. 444.

25. V. Parker, *The Making of King's Lynn*, (1971), plates 40A & 41.

26. **Pevsner,Surrey**, pp. 42-43.

27. **GM** vol. 68, p.763.

28. **M&B**, vol I, p. 349, note 'f' (referring to a Grammar School rental that has since disappeared).

29. *Middlesex Pedigrees*, (Harleian Society, vol 65).

30. **PRO** E179/188/481.

31. *Calendar of the Committee for the Advance of Money*, vol. I, p. 282.

32. **PRO** E179/188/496.

33. Friends Library, Abraham mss., no. 9 (letter of 21st. November 1664 from John Rous to Margaret Fell). I am grateful to the library staff for their help and guidance in connection with this part of the paper.

34. *ibid.*, no. 14.

35. **DNB.**

36. M. Webb, *The Fells of Swarthmore*, (2nd ed., 1896), p. 417.

37. *The Journal of George Fox*, ed. J.L.Nichalls, (1952), pp. 669, 681.

38. J. S. L. Pulford, *The First Kingston Quakers*, (1973), pp. 36-38. For general background, see I. Ross, *Margaret Fell, Mother of Quakerism*, (1949); H. G. Crossfield, *Margaret Fell of Swarthmoor Hall*, (1913).

39. *Journal of the Friends Historical Society*, vol 4, (1907), p. 51; **KBR** KF1/1/44.

40. **Brayley**, vol III, p. 46.

41. **DNB.**

42. For Tillotson's portrait, see **KHC** file prints vol. 11, p. 2(K1-327).

43. **KBR** KD8/2/1; KH1/1/3.

44. **KHC** Pamphlets, vol 26.

45. John Rous was assessed here for poor rate in 1694: **KBR** KG3/2/2.

46. For a general account of the town charities, see **Sampson**, pp. 84-89.

47. A. Anderson, *History and Antiquities of Kingston*, (1818), p. 66.

48. **KBR** KB23/1/1.

49. See H. B. Fant in **SAC**, vol. 47, (1941), pp. 52 ff. I am grateful to Mrs. A. Baker of **KHC** for this reference.

50. **SRO** 331/3/5a-b.

51. [See above, Paper X ('The Three Coneys') and, below, Paper XII for other early examples of brick-built houses.]

52. **PRO** MH12.12390.

53. **KBR** KB9/1.

54. **KBR** KE2/5/1.

55. **Biden**, p. 75.

56. G. Wakefield, *Memoirs*, (1804), vol. I, p. 42.

57. *ibid.*

58. E.Gibbon, *Memories of My Life*, ed. B. Radice, (1984), pp. 64-65.

59. G. Wakefield, *op. cit.*, vol I.

60. *ibid.*, p. 16.

61. **DNB.**

62. **PRO** MH12.12390. [For the earlier workhouse at Surbiton, see **KBR** KG3/4/1, and for the use of the pest-house as a workhouse, see above, Paper IX.]

63. See the appendix to this paper.

64. **KBR** KC1/1/146.

65. **Biden**, p. 94, note 'a'; **SRO** 58/1.

66. **Sampson**, pp. 70-71. There is a copy of the report in **BL** Ref 8275.cc.15i.

67. **PRO** MH12.12389; 12390.

XII

GROVE LODGE, FORMERLY GROVE FARM

[This paper was drafted in 1986 for Mr. P. Cushing, owner of the property, on the basis of deeds supplied by him, and with architectural advice from Mr. I. J. West. It testifies to Miss Wakeford's willingness to devote time and energy, often at the expense of her own work schedule, to helping those whose enthusiasm for historical knowledge was frustrated by lack of technical expertise and practical research experience. Her role as an 'authority' on Kingston's history became increasingly important over the years, and she was frequently consulted not only by individual property owners but also by those engaged in independent study. In the latter context, as her working notes show, she was a substantial (if at her own request, often anonymous) influence on a number of recent local publications.]

The story of Grove Farm and Grove Lodge, so far as it can be gathered from an examination of the house, and from maps and such documents as have survived, is of considerable interest {1}. Although it was until fairly recently well outside the built-up area of the town, it may be said to reflect nearly three centuries of the life of Kingston upon Thames. The house is older than it looks. This often happens, since in the past it was much more usual to adapt and extend than to demolish and rebuild. The alterations known to have been made in the last forty years to provide more accommodation have continued a process begun probably a hundred years or so earlier.

The Building

Ignoring those changes of the twentieth century, Grove Lodge looks like a substantial Victorian residence, with a coach-house such as a gentleman's house then commonly had. But Ayliffe, describing it in 1914 as the house of Dr. Owen, could still recognise the building as 'Miller's Farm', which he remembered from the time of Queen Victoria's coronation in 1837 {2}. At its core still exists a smaller brick-built house with a plan typical of a farmhouse of the late-seventeenth century, dating perhaps from about 1700. Maps of that date are not on a large enough scale for individual small buildings to be identified, nor have any early title deeds for the farm been traced, but the construction of the house tells its own story. The earliest part is two-storeyed plus attics and with a cellar under the south-east corner. The central four-flue chimney stack is characteristic of the late-seventeenth century, and the staircase, although rebuilt, is evidently in its original central position (and for

72

this reason appears rather unimposing for the stairs of a Victorian gentleman's house). There were two rooms on each floor; the kitchen was on the west side, where the room has a solid floor, with a parlour on the other side. Locally made field bricks were used for the walls and oak joists for the floors. The main entrance was on the south side, through the farm-yard, and so, when an enlargement of the house became necessary, a single-storeyed brick extension was built on the opposite side, towards Lower Marsh Lane. This happened in the eighteenth century, probably not very long after the house was built, but is difficult to date because details have been removed, or obscured by later building. There was a chimney between the two new rooms. The work (and also the original house) cannot be dated from documents, because the Kingston rate-books, which sometimes give clues to alterations to houses, are missing for most of the early eighteenth century. However, there was a change of tenant about 1737, when the farm, then belonging to a Leonard Hammond Esq. (who also owned the estate called 'Elmers' at Surbiton) was rated as 'the house and land late Thorp's, to which the collector has added 'now Mr. Warde's' {3}. Perhaps the extension was built by or for the new tenant. After this, the house seems to have been little altered until it ceased to be a farmhouse in the mid-nineteenth century. John Rocque's 1745 map of the area around London is the earliest in which the farmhouse in Lower Marsh Lane is shown, and it had a long barn on the west side. It seems that there were orchards or hop-gardens on either side of the buildings. The two buildings look much the same about a century later in the Kingston Tithe map of about 1840. At that time the one-acre meadow on the west side is called 'Orchard' and a field to the south of it is called 'Great Barn Field' {4}.

The Farm: Owners and Tenants

Two window tax assessments, for 1774 and 1779, have survived. They show that the occupier of the farmhouse, John Smith, had to pay the basic yearly amount of 3s., indicating that the house had fewer than seven windows. This is reasonably consistent with the house after the addition of the single-storey extension {5}. Ayliffe says that in the 1830s large fields of hops were cultivated on Miller's Farm {6}. It is known that in 1838 James Miller was tenant of a small brewery and a malthouse in the Apple Market-Union Street part of Kingston {7}. It seems likely that through the eighteenth and nineteenth centuries Grove Farm grew hops or barley, for there is nearly always an association between the owners or tenants of the farm and the brewing and malting which were Kingston's principal industries. From about 1737 to 1773 the tenants were named Thomas Ward (father and son), who had malthouses in Kingston {8}. Towards the end of the eighteenth century, and later, the Westbrooke family were tenants. They seem to have had links with various inns in the town, including the Nag's Head, a very old place (called the Rose in Tudor times) which had its own small brewery. This inn can still be seen, though mutilated, as Nos. 6-8 Church Street, Kingston {9}.

There is some information about the various landlords, the owners of the farm. The first definitely known, the Leonard Hammond who had it in 1737, was one of three generations of that family (all called Leonard) who had owned the 'Elmers' estate at Surbiton from about 1662. Possibly the Grove Farm lands had been part of Elmers, but when Leonard Hammond sold the house and lands called Elmers to Peregrine Fury in 1742, he kept the smaller farm which Thomas Ward had held {10}. In December 1745 he sold it to a Kingston brewer, Richard Welbrough (or Welborough). This sale led later to another interesting grouping of properties. At just about the same time Walter Kent, Esq. died. He was a former High Sheriff of Surrey and a Kingston landowner. Among other properties, he owned, and had occupied for over forty years, the house and small estate called The Grove (adjoining Grove Farm), on part of which Kingston Polytechnic now stands. In 1740 he had made his will, leaving most of his Kingston property, including the Grove, to his servant Jane Morris {11}. By the time of his death in 1746 Jane had married another Kingston brewer, John Tickner. He must have died very soon, for on 8th. October 1748, she made a settlement on her marriage to Richard Welbrough, dealing with the property left to her by her former employer Walter Kent {11}. So the two properties, The Grove and Grove Farm, were owned by the wife and husband, and after Jane's death (there were evidently no children of their marriage) by Richard Welbrough alone. On his death in December 1765 his daughter Elizabeth Adams inherited both, together with other properties which Jane had settled {12}. As a married woman, Elizabeth Adams could not hold property so her husband Richard was owner in her right.

At this time, Grove Farm is referred to in the Land Tax books as 'farm in the Marsh' {13}. Grove Lane was Lower Marsh Lane until the nineteenth century. The whole area was called 'The Marsh' right up to the development of modern Surbiton (after the coming of the railway in 1838). In the Middle Ages it was Marshfield, one the great arable fields of Surbiton. It must once have been marshland of the Hogsmill (in early times probably a much more important river), later perhaps dairy pastures, before the land became dry enough for ploughing {14}. The Kingston properties of Richard Adams later descended to Richard Gray, whose heirs put them up for sale by auction in 1836. The Sale Particulars have not survived, but the sketch-map which evidently went with them is in the Surrey Record Office {15}. The fields of Grove Farm are shown as nos. 9 and 16. For some years in the 1820s and 1830s, the Grove Farm tenant had been W. S. Minchin (who had interests in farm and market-garden land in other parts of Kingston and in Hampton Wick). In 1838 it was still referred to as Minchin's Farm, though by that time the farmer was the James Miller already mentioned {16}. Miller bought the farm soon afterwards, for in the tithe apportionment book of 1842 he is shown as owner-occupier of the house and of the 40 acres of arable and meadow land around it, shown in the 1838 plan {17}. This was probably much the same as the farm of a century earlier. James Miller also farmed (as tenant) a further 43 acres in the Marsh, on the other side of Villiers Road, and he owned and occupied another house somewhere in the Brighton Road area of Surbiton. This may be why Grove farmhouse is shown in the 1841 census return as occupied only by Mr. Miller himself and one servant. Presumably he used it just for the purpose of overseeing the farm work {18}.

Modern Changes

James Miller left the farm about 1846. The first railway line through the Kingston area had been opened in 1838 and the new Surbiton was growing up round the railway station there. This must have changed the prospects of Grove Farm. That is probably why most of the farmland was sold, separately from the house, to Mr. C. E. Jemmett, the Town Clerk of Kingston, to join to the considerable estate which he already owned in what is now the Cranes Park area of Surbiton, where he had a substantial house of that name {19}. But the slowness of the development is shown on the map with the Sale Particulars when the Cranes Park Estate was being sold as building land in 1888 {20}. By that time Edward Grove (whose executors were selling) had bought both Grove Lodge from Mr. Powell and the Cranes Park Estate from the Jemmett family in 1875, shortly before his own death. Meanwhile the old farmhouse of about 1700 had taken on a new character as Grove Lodge. The house with land for gardens and paddock was bought by 1848 by James B. E. Soden. According to the 1851 census return, he was a half-pay R.N. Purser, who lived there with his wife, eleven-year-old daughter and one servant {21}. From this time Grove Lodge no longer houses small farmers and brewers, but the larger households of more substantial residents, requiring increased accommodation and a general upgrading of the house and grounds. Alterations can be traced on maps and in the fabric of the house itself.

In 1851 the Chelsea Waterworks Co, deposited with the Surrey Justices of the Peace a plan and reference book concerning their proposed pipe-line from their new reservoir on the Thames at Surbiton, near Seething Wells, to another reservoir on Putney Heath {22}. The land required for the pipeline included part of the grounds of Grove Lodge. The plans shows the same small house. The long barn has gone, replaced by the beginning of a footpath (now Beaufort Road) leading to the Waggon and Horses at the foot of Surbiton Hill Road, and so on to the railway station. A little construction on the south wall of Grove Lodge shown in this 1851 plan tells us that the porch had already been built to dignify the old farmhouse entrance, and a detached coach house/stable had been built at the north-west corner of the property, adjoining Lower Marsh Lane. Ten years later the 1861 census gives a much bigger household at Grove Lodge {23}. Its head is Mr. James Powell, described as 'landed proprietor', born in Kent and having lived at Lingfield, Surrey. There are his three children, aged 21, 18 and one year (the last born in Kingston), a young nephew, and three women servants. About 1864 Kingston was surveyed for the first large-scale Ordnance Survey maps. The maps show that the house had been extended to accommodate this family. It was probably at this time that the roof of the old house was raised and the pitch slackened to cover the extension, now two-storeyed, on the north side {24}. The extension is shown on these maps, and so are the bay windows added on either side of the original house.

At the 1886 sale, Grove Lodge was offered with 'an exceedingly valuable plot of freehold building land', described as 'ripe for immediate development'. The total area of the Grove Lodge property was stated as 8 acres and 3 roods {25}. It seems, however, that the building land, to the east along Grove Lane, was sold separately, for Edward Grove's executors, by a conveyance of 28th. October 1889, sold the house, coach-house, gardens and small paddock (running along Beaufort Road), a total of only 3 roods and 18 perches, to Robert and Thomas S. Lamb for £1,200 {26}. Probably the gardens had been laid out more than 25 years before for Mr. James Powell. The lawns, shrubberies and flower-beds of a typical Victorian gentleman's garden are shown in detail in the 1864 Ordnance Survey map, with a kitchen garden to the east of the house and a paddock with trees, running along the (then still unnamed) Beaufort Road. A small house, next along Grove Lane to the east, was the home (according to the 1861 census) of Henry Wood, 'gentleman gardener'. As he and his wife had been born at Lingfield, like Mr. Powell's daughter and one of his servants, presumably Henry Wood was the gardener at Grove Lodge. The census does not show a coachman or groom living over the coach-house at that time. After the 1889 conveyance, members of the Lamb family occupied the house for more than ten years. In 1902 it was bought by Harry Harden Esq., for £1,500 and he moved there from Richmond Road, Kingston. In 1915 he sold it to J. G. Owen, surgeon, who already lived there {27}.

The development of this house from a small farmhouse, probably serving the local brewing and malting industries, to a gentleman's residence with no connection with trade or industry, and then to the home and premises of a professional man, all without drastic demolition and rebuilding, has in the past been typical of the English process of 'evolution not revolution', other examples of which are found in Kingston and in many other places. The history of Grove Farm, Grove Lodge, 2 Grove Lane, is part of the history of Kingston upon Thames - and of England.

Appendix: -- Grove Lodge -- was it a duke's shooting-box ? {28}

The story that Grove Lodge had been a 'shooting-box' of the Duke of Beaufort, or perhaps of the Duke of Buckingham seems to be of modern origin, as it is not mentioned by Victorian or earlier local historians (in fact I have never seen it in print). The association may have been suggested by the present road-names in the vicinity. The Dukes of Buckingham are not known to have had any interests in the Kingston area. The local road and public house names connected with this family are Victorian or later, inspired by the history of the death in 1648 of the 'beautiful Francis Villiers', the Duke's brother, on Surbiton Hill in the last skirmish of the Civil War {29}. Grove Lodge is on the corner of Beaufort Road, but the house existed long before the road, which was only a footpath in 1851. I have not found any reason for the name Beaufort, here and elsewhere in the Kingston neighbourhood (e.g. Beaufort Road, Ham; Beaufort Villa, a Victorian house in Knight's Park, Kingston, in local directories from 1866). If the 'shooting-box' story already existed and had given rise to the road name, it is surprising that Biden's well-known local history does not mention it. The dukedom of Beaufort was created in 1682 for Henry Somerset, third Marquess of Worcester, a descendant of a fifteenth-century illegitimate son of Henry Beaufort, Duke of Somerset {30}. Even if a house existed on the site in 1682, the rate books of the period do not include these names. From 1737 the owners and occupiers of the house are known and (as has been shown) it is referred to as a farmhouse and rated with its lands. The best-known earlier bearer of the name Beaufort was Cardinal Beaufort, Bishop of Winchester, half-brother of

XXXVII. Norbiton Lodge, 1907. The property stood on the southern side of London Road as it approaches the junction with Coombe Road, and belonged to C. M. Westmacott in 1840. The castellated effect on the right of the picture is reminiscent of the architecture of nos. 155/157 London Road. (**KHC** file print K1-715).

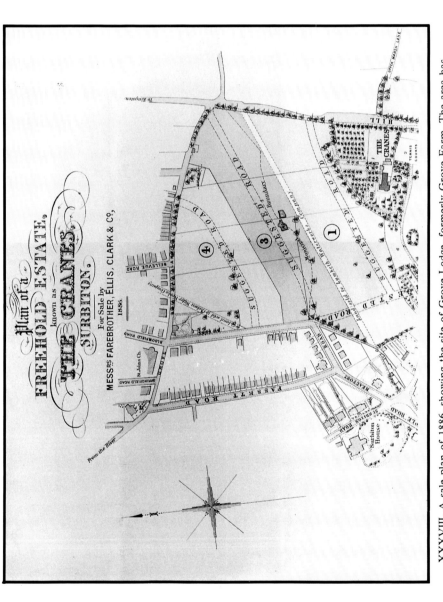

XXXVIII. A sale plan of 1886, showing the site of Grove Lodge, formerly Grove Farm. The area has clearly already been marked down for further development. (**SRO SP 9/45/1**).

Henry IV. He lived from 1370 to 1447, three centuries before Grove Lodge was built, and neither he nor the Beaufort Duke of Somerset is known to have had any connection with the land. However, there is no certain information about the site at such an early date. From 1663 it was apparently treated as part of Leonard Hammond's Elmers Farm, which was formerly (from about 1376) an endowment of the London Charterhouse and is not known to have been let to any of the Beauforts.

1. The current address is No. 2, Grove Lane, Kingston upon Thames.

2. **Ayliffe**, p. 46.

3. **KBR** KG3/2/7.

4. **SRO** P33/2/1. (plots 646, 647, 648).

5. **KBR** KD8/3/1; 8/3/2.

6. **Ayliffe**, p. 46.

7. **SRO** 474 (no. 781).

8. **KBR** KG3/2/7.

9. For early references to 'The Rose', see **KBR** KC1/1/131; 1/1/134; 1/1/135.

10. **SRO** 176/20/1.

11. **KBR** KF1/1/84; **SRO** 521.

12. **KBR** KF1/1/104.

13. It is thus described, e.g., in **SRO** QS6/7 (1792 Land Tax).

14. **SRO** 266/9/1/26-27.

15. **SRO** 494/1.

16. A. Raphael is named as the owner in 1838: **SRO** 474 (no. 781).

17. **SRO** P33/2/1 (plots 646-649, 653-657).

18. 1841 Census (microfilm in **KHC**).

19. **SRO** 262/9/1.

20. **SRO** SP9/45/1.

21. 1851 Census (microfilm in **KHC**).

22. **SRO** QS6/8/420.

23. 1861 Census (microfilm in **KHC**).

24. This is the view of Mr. I. J. West.

25. **SRO** SP9/45/1.

26. Deed supplied by Mr. P. Cushing, the owner of the property. [There is a summary in **KBR** KX79/67.]

27. *ibid.*

28. The issue of the duke's shooting-box is separately treated to avoid confusion.

29. **Sampson**, pp. 32-33.

30. *Handbook of British Chronology*, ed. F. M. Powicke and E. B. Fryde, (2nd. ed., 1961), pp. 417, 449.

XIII

'ELMFIELD', LONDON ROAD

[This paper, dated 1975, was written for The Tiffinian *(the magazine of the Tiffin School in Kingston) published in December of that year. As on other occasions, Miss Wakeford had the benefit of expert architectural advice from Mr. I. J. West.]*

Elmfield, now the Sixth Form Centre of the Tiffin School, and its oldest building, is the last survivor of the days when Norbiton was full of fine mansions {1}. In the eighteenth century, the building was a gentleman's residence called Walnut Tree House, and in the early nineteenth century became 'a very respectable school for gentlemen' known as Walnut Tree Academy, run by a Dr. Harcourt. But when Brayley wrote his county history in about 1840, the house was still remembered as 'once the residence of the ill-fated Capt. Richard Pierce, who, with a great part of his family, was lost in the *Halsewell* East-Indiaman off Portland, about sixty years ago' {2}. This tragic shipwreck caused a great stir in its time and is described in a vivid contemporary account {3}. For those interested in sailing ships the details given of the handling of the 758-ton East-Indiaman in the terrible weather of January 1786 are worth reading. The ship was taking soldiers to the Company's garrisons in Asia and also (the distinction is significant) eight 'respectable passengers' of whom seven were young officers and wealthy merchants of the Company's Indian stations. A Mr. Miller had been engaged by Captain Pierce to superintend his 'band of music' and to accompany the young ladies on the pianoforte. Captain Pierce was said to have had 'great taste in the polite arts' and on a previous voyage had taken the painter Zoffany out to India, where he obtained many commissions. The captain was the oldest serving East India Company commander and had evidently settled at Walnut Tree House in 1781 in preparation for his retirement. He had brought back at least one servant from his travels for Kingston Parish records the baptism on 16th. January 1785 of Lucy Duncombe 'a black from Captain Peirce's' {4}.

The *Halsewell* sailed from Gravesend on New Year's Day, 1786, almost immediately met gales and snowstorms, and in the early morning darkness of Friday, 6th. January, struck and broke up on the rocky coast of the Isle of Purbeck. Of more than 240 who had sailed in her, only 73 (18 officers, 30 seamen and 25 soldiers) survived. Captain Pierce, his two daughters and two nieces were all lost and the chief mate, Thomas Burston of Kingston, decided to die with 'his cousins, the Miss Pierces, for were he to leave such dear relatives behind, he could only expect the worst of deaths, to be discarded for ever from the service'. The captain, hearing that there was no way to rescue the girls, enfolded his daughters in his arms and said, 'Thus, my dear children, we will perish together'. These affecting stories naturally made a deep impression and one suspects some exaggeration in the high-flown eighteenth-century obituary notices. However, Captain Pierce seems to have been an amiable and accomplished gentleman and it was sad that 'he did not live to enjoy the "competent fortune" which he had accumulated and his honorable retirement in his elegant house'.

An earlier house on the Elmfield site had probably been a gentleman's residence from at any rate the 1680s, but it had once been a farm, called the Chapel farm because it had belonged to the neighbouring Lovekyn Chantry Chapel, though it did not form part of the subsequent endowment made over to the Grammar School in Queen Elizabeth's day {5}. In 1738 the house was bought by a London gentleman with the splendidly eighteenth century name of Peregrine Fury, Esq. {6}. The property was then described as a capital messuage, barns, stables, coach houses, dovehouse, room and granary under the dovehouse, outhouses, etc., with nine acres of land adjoining and also the farmyard lately converted into a garden, whereon two barns lately stood, all in Norbiton street near the Free Grammar School in Kingston. There was also a pew in Kingston Church. The Furys were a military family and the purchaser of the house was secretary to Chelsea Royal Hospital {7}. He died in 1759, but the property continued in his family until 1825 {8}.

The house he bought was often let, usually for short terms to wealthy tenants. In 1747/48, for example, it was occupied by Admiral Martin, who had just retired and later settled at the more fashionable Twickenham. It was said of the Admiral that 'he not only possessed a considerable share of classical learning, but spoke the French, Spanish, Italian and German languages with the greatest ease and fluency. In his person he was remarkably handsome and particularly attentive to his dress, manners and deportment. When in command he lived in the greatest splendour, maintaining his rank in the highest style.' {9}. Soon after, the tenant was the Lady Selina Bathurst, the recently widowed daughter of Earl Ferrers. She was succeeded by the wealthy Robert Linch Bloss, heir to an Irish baronetcy: as his wife had recently died, he also may have been seeking another permanent establishment in the neighbourhood.

We do not know what sort of house these eminent personages rented: it can hardly have been the timbered farmhouse of Tudor times and one may guess that like other big houses in Norbiton and Coombe it had been rebuilt in red brick in the mid-seventeenth century {10}. In the early Georgian period it became fashionable to think red brick too glaring and to use yellow stock bricks for new houses: Mr. Fury's town house in Great Pulteney Street had a front of pale yellow stock brick and he rebuilt his Kingston house in the same bricks in 1756/57 {11}. There are two early nineteenth century pictures of Walnut Tree House in the British Library {12}. They show that the present Elmfield is substantially the same house, with some alterations and additions; in particular, the main door was formerly in the centre of the angled bay, so that the present library with its interesting screen at the inner end was originally the hall. The fine quality of much of the interior can still be appreciated; for example, the fanlight over one of the first-floor doors, the stairs and some of the fireplaces (which are probably later than the original house). An unusual feature is the opening panels under a sashed window on the ground floor {13}. The house was assessed to Window Tax in 1774 for

79

56 windows and by this criterion was one of the eight largest in Kingston {14}. Mr. Fury probably had the gardens laid out with fashionable lawns when the house was rebuilt, for in 1785 he was fined by Kingston manorial court for cutting a large quantity of turf on Norbiton Common and so spoiling the grazing for commoners' beasts {15}.

Mr. Fury' s son, also Peregrine, was married in Kingston Church in 1762 to Miss Ann Greenly of Norbiton Hall {16}. He lived in the new house until 1773, but also had a town house in Grosvenor Street. At the time of his death in 1792 he was one of the gentlemen of His Majesty's Privy Chamber and he had probably left Kingston in favour of Richmond or Kew to be near the Court {17}. After this the house was let and in 1775/76 the tenant was another newly-married man, the fourth Duke of Atholl, then only twenty years old. Soon afterwards Captain Pierce, who had lived elsewhere in Kingston for about twenty years, took the mansion.

The large square one-storeyed extension at the back of the house seems to be a Victorian kitchen. The Census returns of the middle decades of the nineteenth century show the staff then needed to run a house of this size. In 1841 an East India merchant lived at Walnut Tree House with his wife, three children and their governess and with five female and two male servants living in. By 1851 it was again a school, now for young ladies. The Misses Compton (aged 57 and 50), with an assistant teacher and a French governess from Rouen, had four female servants to look after sixteen 'gentlewomen' boarders, aged from 9 to 18, some of whom had been born in India {18}.

The 1827 picture of Walnut Tree Academy shows the house almost dwarfed by a great tree which must have been an elm, for by 1861 the walnut tree had been forgotten and the name was The Elms, the home of a retired clergyman, his two sisters and his barrister nephew, with the nephew's wife and little girl. This household was attended by five women servants (one aged 74) and there was also a footman living in. It must be remembered that there will almost certainly have been outdoor servants (gardeners, a coachman and a groom, for example) not living in the house {19}. The contrast with those palmy days is striking, but Kingston is fortunate that a modern use has been found for the mansion and that instead of being demolished, it is well-maintained and so little altered. The Tiffin School must be proud to be custodians of this fine and interesting house.

1. I am grateful to Mr. L. Wallis of the Tiffin School for arranging access to the house and to Mr. I. J. West who accompanied me and gave expert advice about the building's architecture.

2. **Brayley**, vol III, p. 39.

3. *Annual Register*, vol. 28, (1786), pp. 224-233 (copy in **KHC**). [This work forms the basis of the following account, but individual references are not separately footnoted.]

4. **KPR(B)** 16th. January 1785.d.

5. Chapel Farm was sold to Thomas Locke in 1553: **CPR** Edward VI, vol. V, pp. 194-95.

6. **SRO** 270/3a-b; 270/4.

7. **GM** vol. 13, (1743), p. 218.

8. **KPR(B)** 20th. September 1759; **GM** vol. 29, (1759), p. 497. His will is in **PRO** PROB 11 849/326. William Mercer is shown as owner in 1826: **SRO** QS6/7(Land Tax).

9. **DNB**.

10. [For another example, see above, Paper XI.]

11. Survey of London. vol. XXXI: *Parish of St. James, Westminster, Part II., North of Piccadilly*, (1963), p. 132.

12. **M&B(Percival)**, vol V, after p.404 (dating from the 1820s).

13. The architectural description owes much to the judgements of Mr. I. J. West. For a fuller account, see **DBRG(S)**, No. 1114.

14. **KBR** KD8/3/1.

15. **KBR** KF1/9/93.

16. National Library of Wales, Ms. 268.

17. His will is in **PRO** PROB 11 1214/72. See also, **GM** vol. 62, (1792), p. 184.

18. 1851 Census (microfilm in **KHC**).

19. 1861 Census (microfilm in **KHC**)

XIV

KINGSTON HILL PLACE

[This paper, dated February 1985 and found among Miss Wakeford's working notes, takes as its starting point an early-nineteenth-century illustration preserved in Percival's grangerized version of Manning and Bray's well-known county history {1}. This is a work of considerable value, containing a large number of original prints and sketches relating to the Kingston area (as indeed to most of the villages and townships of Surrey), but has not been much used by local historians in the past. Miss Wakeford's interest in the collection should be seen as part of her broader strategy for making more consistent use of all surviving pictorial evidence for Kingston's past. Her frequent recourse to the substantial collection of old Kingston photographs in Kingston Heritage Centre, and to a lesser extent those in back numbers of the Surrey Comet, *have the same underlying motivation.]*

The earliest known illustrations of the house are two coloured drawings in the British Library copy of Manning and Bray's *The History of the County of Surrey*, grangerized by Percival {1}. One bears the inscription 'On Kingston Common - Robert Lawes Esq. - J. Stokes 1830' and is a view from the road, showing gates to a drive, with a low wooden fence to the right. The other is obviously by the same artist and shows the house from a little further down the road, looking over the fence. The reference to Kingston Common is an understandable mistake; the site at this early date was evidently still recognisable as common or waste land, but belonged to the manor of Ham, being separated from the better-known Ham Common by the land enclosed in Richmond Park.

Robert Lawes of Wimbledon Common, Esq., had acquired the house and land in 1829 for £4,060 at public auction, when the estate was sold by the trustees in bankruptcy of Samuel Baxter the elder, a London builder. They conveyed it to Lawes by a deed of 25th. August 1829, recorded as Ham manor court of 11th. July 1838 {2}. The estate (which ran down between the main road and the Park from the top of the hill for about two-thirds of a mile) was a patchwork of pieces of land acquired by Samuel Baxter the elder from different sources. Although no title deeds have been traced, a plan showing the various pieces was filed with the record of a Special Court Baron of Ham manor held on 29th. October 1828 {3}. On this plan the house is shown for the first time, standing on land which was formerly the site of the old road from London to Portsmouth. A plan of this land, bought for £350 by Samuel Baxter of Regent Street, London, builder, from the turnpike commissioners, and conveyed to him on 19th. April 1827, is in the Quarter Sessions record for 15th. January 1828 {4}. There was then no house there. It must therefore have been built between April 1827 and October 1828 by

Samuel Baxter the elder. The architect, if any, would not be mentioned in records of this type.

A document of 1829 among Kingston Borough records shows that Samuel Baxter (now described as a builder of Tottenham Court Road, London) granted to Samuel Oxenham of Oxford Street, auctioneer, a one-year lease of his old road land, with nine acres of land in Coombe lying between the lines of the old and new roads {5}. These two pieces are the only freehold land which Baxter owned there, and such a lease would normally be the first step in a conveyance of the freeholds to Oxenham. Baxter evidently intended to sell the new house, but the second document is missing, and in any case Baxter's imminent bankruptcy may well have invalidated any attempted sale. Oxenham was, however, made a party to the conveyance of 25th. August 1829 to Robert Lawes, probably to release any claim he may have had to the freeholds. According to the Ham manor court record of 29th. October 1828, the freehold land in Coombe had been 'lately' bought by Baxter from Earl Spencer, then lord of the manor of Coombe {6}.

At Ham manor court of 14th. July 1827, Baxter had been admitted as copyhold tenant of 2 acres 2 roods and 26 perches of land between the old road and the Park wall which had formerly belonged to Philip Cawston, the landlord of the Robin Hood Inn {7}. This land was acquired (probably some time in the half-year before the court) by Baxter from persons claiming to be entitled to it under the will of Cawston's widow, Sarah, on her death in 1825. One of them was Baxter's son, Samuel Baxter the younger; presumably the London builder's interest in the development potential of the land on 'Robin Hood Hill' arose from his son's acquisition, for the father then lost no time in putting together his substantial estate there. At the Ham court baron of 29th. October 1828 he was admitted as copyhold tenant of the rest of the waste between the old road land and the Park wall, with the two other pieces of waste alongside the old road, thus completing the grounds of Kingston Hill Place {8}. With so much land, Baxter must have meant to build more than one house, but he was probably short of capital for the enterprise. The land granted to him on 28th. October 1828 was immediately mortgaged to Benjamin Bernard, Esq. for £200 at 5%. This loan was repaid on 21st. August 1829 by the commissioners in the bankruptcy of Samuel Baxter the elder, who by that time had died.

After the sale of Baxter's estate on Kingston Hill to Robert Lawes, his title to the 2 acres 2 roods and 26 perches of copyhold land was challenged by Mrs. Mary Winder, one of Philip Cawston's customary heirs, on highly technical grounds involving the terms of the wills of the Cawston family, the customs of Ham manor, and the formalities required for making title to copyholds. In June 1837 judgement was given in an action of ejectment and, as the result was partly against Robert Lawes, formal steps had to be taken and recorded at Ham court baron on 11th. July 1838 to restore his legal position (only £100 of the £4,060 which he had paid for the estate was apportioned to the Ham copyholds) {9}.

Investigation of the records has shown how a London builder saw the possibilities of the land, put together an estate, and built a gentleman's house in 1827/8 - and bankrupted himself in the process. The irony is that, although his own operations outran his resources, Baxter's vision must have stimulated the second and third Earls Spencer to develop their land on the opposite side opposite side of the road. In 1832 and 1835 building leases of part of Coombe Woods were granted and the houses now called Kenry House and Coombe Hurst (both also now housing Kingston Polytechnic) were built for William Ogle Hunt and Samuel Smith, Esq., the latter the uncle of Florence Nightingale, who often stayed at Coombe Hurst {10}. These three fine houses were the first substantial residences built on Kingston Hill, each with beautiful pleasure grounds. Thus Samuel Baxter, though personally unsuccessful, was influential in setting the standard for the area for many years to come.

1. This important work was first drawn to the attention of **KUTAS** by Mr. R. Taylor in a lecture entitled 'Percival's Kingston'. The lecture is reported in **KUTAS CHRONICLE** (March 1973).

2 **SRO** 58/2/2/3, p. 147.

3. *ibid.,* p.88.

4. **SRO** QS2/1/48.

5. **KBR** KX12. I am grateful to the Kingston Assistant Borough archivist both for this and the preceding reference.

6. **SRO** 58/2/2/3, p. 90.

7. *ibid.*

8. *ibid.*

9. *ibid.*

10. L. E. Gent, *The Manor of Coombe or Coombe Nevill,* (**KUTAS** Occasional Paper No. 3, 1979), p. 12.

XXXIX. An early but undated sketch of 'Elmfield', London Road. Formerly known as Walnut Tree House, the building survives as part of the Tiffin school. (**BL** CRACH 1.Tab.1.b.1., vol. V, following p. 404).

XL. A view of Kingston Hill Place 1830 by J. Stokes. The reference to Kingston Common is misleading in legal if not environmental terms: the land here was waste of the manor of Ham. (**BL** CRACH.1.Tab.1.b.1., vol. V, following p. 406).

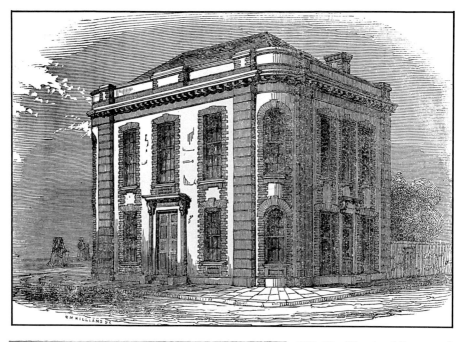

XLI. The Kingston Literary and Scientific Institution, as depicted on the front cover of Seeley's Miscellany for 1841. An early work of Gilbert Scott, the building survived until the recent Horse Fair development programme. (**KHC** Local History Collection).

XLII. W. E. St.L. Finny as Mayor of Kingston 1898. His political commitment was matched by a keen interest in the archaeology and early history of the town. (**KHC** file print K1-2253).

XV

THE KINGSTON LITERARY AND SCIENTIFIC INSTITUTION (7-9 CLARENCE STREET)

[This paper first appeared in KUTAS NL *(No. 9, June 1981) and like other examples of Miss Wakeford's work was written in response to the imminent destruction of an interesting local building. The source from which much of the information is taken,* Seeley's Kingston Miscellany, *has long been available in Kingston Heritage Centre, but Miss Wakeford is the first local writer to realise its potential. The value of the paper is enhanced by the fact that Miss Wakeford rarely concerned herself with Victorian buildings, though in general (as some of her topographical studies show) she was well aware of the important changes taking place in the physical lay-out of the town in the nineteenth century.]*

The Horse Fair development has meant the demolition of these premises of our Victorian predecessors, the Kingston Literary and Scientific Institution, and the end of the story which began with high hopes in 1839. Its early course may be followed in a short-lived monthly magazine called *Seeley's Kingston Miscellany*. The engraving of the newly-built premises was the frontispiece of the 1841 volume, covering the first two years of this publication {1}.

The Building

The objects of the Institute were 'The promotion and diffusion of useful knowledge in Literature, Science and the Arts; by means of a Reading Room -- Library of Reference -- Circulating Library -- Lecture-Meetings at which Essays and Original Papers will be read and discussed -- the formation of Classes for Study -- and the collection of Apparatus and a Museum'. The Institution needed suitable premises for these ambitious plans and fortunately a benefactor appeared in the person of Dr. George Taylor, a popular G. P., much interested in the working classes. He provided a lease of a vacant plot of land opposite his other property (his residence on the north side of the Bridge approach was until recent demolition the back part of the furniture shop on the corner of Thames Street and the Bridge approach). He also gave £ 1, 800 for the building and, as he was on the committee which had recently chosen the architects Scott and Moffatt for St. Peter' s Church, Norbiton, the same firm was appointed for this building, which was begun in September

1840. Scott and Moffatt was a partnership formed by George Gilbert Scott (then in his twenties) to make a rather humdrum living designing workhouses in the Elizabethan style for the new Poor Law Unions. At this time the town of Kingston consisted mainly of old timber-framed and weather-boarded buildings and the go-ahead founders of the Institute stipulated that their premises should look quite different. The architects, perhaps thinking of a small version of a London club, suggested the Wren style still just perceptible in the building on the eve of its demolition. The result was considered a striking building, 'remarkable not merely for its general structure, but from the peculiarity of the materials used', namely yellow bricks for the flat parts and red for those which projected. The Institute could not afford to take the whole building so the engraving tactfully leaves the other tenant's Clarence Street frontage in shadow.

On 15th. October 1841 the new building was opened by holding there the Institution's second anniversary meeting. The proceedings began with 'an amateur band of Kingston instrumentalists' leading off and Dr. Taylor handed over the key to the President, Mr. Gould. The Presidential address (on the objects of Science) 'though as lengthy as most "President's Messages" was well received by the meeting' says Mr. Seeley, 'if we may judge by the plaudits that accompanied its delivery'. Mr. Seeley gives a full description of the building. The Lecture Room, 30ft. by 20ft., was on the first floor. It was 16ft. high, warmed by a stove and ventilated by an apparatus in the ceiling, and had a 30ft. gallery for extra seating, approached through the Committee Room. Lecturers had a screen for diagrams, worked by a pulley (Mr. Biden suggested this and supervised its erection). The members proposed to have gas laid on as soon as the Institution could afford the outlay: meanwhile they presumably used Ranyards candles like the rest of Kingston. The Lecture Room could be used also as a reading-room, open to members and subscribers from 10 am. to 5 pm., with newspapers and other leading periodicals (there was of course no public library in Kingston at this time). The Library proper was on the ground floor, to the left of the Thames Street entrance. A catalogue of the books had already been printed and was being sold bound up with the Institution's rules and the President's Annual Address; this interesting publication unfortunately appears not to have survived. In the basement was the Chemical Class Room.

Activities

According to Mr. Seeley, the Chemical Class Room was 'fitted up with an excellent pump, and a suitable grate'. Mr. Biden's lecture on 23rd. March 1841 on the formation and application of the Air Pump, with 'several pleasing experiments', had been considered as the first fruits of the Institution's scientific class, though members (especially Mr. Gould) had evidently been reading many papers to the class itself. They were also collecting £ 10 for the cost of an 'oxy-hydrogen microscope' which they were constructing. A Lexicon of about 1850 indicates that this was an early magic lantern, illuminated by a potentially dangerous combination of oxygen and hydrogen, and presumably used by members to show the results of their researches (the favourite pursuit of the serious-minded at this period was watching the *animalculae* wriggling in samples of ditchwater under a microscope). (see Appendix, below).

A drawing class was also formed and music-lovers had a weekly meeting. Hints were dropped that 'persons should unite' to buy an organ, which would be first lent to, and later bought by the Institution. Members were urged to donate 'specimens' for a Museum and the Treasurer, Mr. Shearman, set an example by presenting -- a case of stuffed birds!

The lecture programme was dominated by a wide variety of scientific subjects, but included also Ancient Greece, modern problems and the Arts -- 'The Philosophy of Machinery', 'Is Emigration Unpatriotic?', 'Climate and Diet', 'Slavery as it is encouraged in the United States', 'Voice', 'Elocution' and 'Parliamentary Eloquence'. The title 'Fossil Fuel' has a modern ring. Two lectures by Mr. Stanesby on Railways and Locomotive Engines 'made what is generally considered a very dry subject prove very interesting as well as instructive'; evidently Kingston was still determinedly indifferent to the new transport, however forward-looking were the Institution's leading members in other ways.

Members

No list of members has survived, but those mentioned include names familiar later as the successful businessmen, 'developers' and civic personalities of Kingston and the new Surbiton. Mr. Benton Seeley, already a Town Councillor, was the first secretary of the Institution, and was soon succeeded by Mr. Biden (presumably of the select Academy for boys in Heathen Street). Other leading members were Mr. Dawson, the auctioneer, the thirty-year-old Mr. Samuel Ranyard (later on the board of the new Kingston Gas Co., and a leader in Surbiton life), Mr. D. Fricker, Mr. W.D. Biden (later the historian of Kingston), and Mr. Edward Phillips the chemist in Thames Street {2}. But Mr. Frederick Gould seems to have been regarded, by others as well as himself, as the founder of the Institution. In the course of his subsequent long public life in Kingston Mr. Gould had a finger in every pie, but at this time he was only 22, newly arrived from Bath to be assistant to Mr. Jones the chemist in the Market Place and shocked to find 'that there was no opportunity for mental improvement on the part of the young men of the town'. He evidently lost no time in remedying the situation and even gas-lighted the Assize Court building in order to use it for the Institution's early lectures. Gas had been introduced into Kingston, against great opposition, only six years earlier. Mr. Gould and the other young innovators must have seemed (to use the modern term) 'activists' indeed to Kingstonians who had grown up before the reforms of the 1830s and who were accustomed to the old self-appointing corporation and to the restrictions of the old Trading Companies.

Though the Institution seemed to be going well (as an old man Mr. Gould told the *Surrey Comet* in 1897 that membership had reached 400), it is evident from *Seeley's Miscellany* that there was local opposition. Poor attendances at some lectures were blamed on the short-sighted local tradesmen, who would not release their employees until after 8 pm. 'You gain gold', Mr. Seeley told the shopkeepers, 'they lose what rubies could not buy'.

It is clear from this that the Institution was intended to benefit the young working-men of the town, but perhaps when these early members began to succeed in their own businesses, an element of class-distinction crept in. By 1852 when Mr. W. D. Biden's history of Kingston was published, he and his friends were meeting as a society of 'a few gentlemen', each of whom engaged to introduce, in his turn, a subject for conversation (politics and theology being excluded) and in the 1850s the fine building was referred to as the Mechanics' Institute. However, the *Surrey Comet and General Advertiser* for 26th. August 1854 had a notice of meetings of the 'Literary Institution' at the Reading Room of the Mechanics' Library and Scientific Institute; particulars were obtainable from Mr. Diamond, the librarian, at the office of the Institution in Church Street (where he had a bookbinding business).

Later Developments

By 1877 when Chapman's *Handbook of Kingston* appeared, his list of local libraries and reading rooms did not include the Institution, but 'young men engaged in business had a reading-room in Brick Lane (now Union Street). The Clarence-Street building was for a while the Leopold Coffee Tavern, a temperance undertaking (perhaps under the patronage of Prince Leopold, Duke of Albany, who lived at Claremont). Later it was a china shop and then a bank. It may be that the commercial uses were a consequence of the expiry of the original lease granted for charitable purposes by Dr. Taylor, who was presumably dead by this time.

When Dr. Finny wrote his *Homeland Handbook* (1902), a Kingston Literary Society was providing weekly in winter 'an attractive programme of scientific and instructive lectures in St. James' Hall'. It is not certain that this was the Institution founded in 1839, though the emphasis on science has a familiar ring {3}.

Surrey Archaeological Society held its first A.G.M. at Kingston Town Hall in 1854 during Mr. Frederick Gould's mayoralty, and heard a talk on the History and Antiquities of Kingston by Mr. Samuel Ranyard, who exhibited the signet ring illustrated in Biden's book of the same name {4}. Mr. Gould was for many years local secretary of Surrey Archaeological Society and soon after his death in 1900 the Society again met in Kingston. His spiritual heir, the young Dr. Finny, showed the members Alderman Gould's collection of antiquities, then at the Technical Institution. The collection may have been later transferred to Kingston Museum, opened in 1904, and if so, must have been among the earliest accessions {5}.

It may also be that Biden's well known history of the town originated in the activities of a group of members of the Kingston Literary and Scientific Institution, for at the end of his *Miscellany* in December 1841, Mr. Seeley said that the History of Kingston, which had been announced on the cover of some of the monthly numbers, 'is in a forward state, and will soon be introduced to our readers' {6}. He added that 'any kind friend who has materials by him, will confer a favour by giving us his assistance'. Perhaps the process of producing the history took longer than anticipated - we may sympathise! Articles on Edmund Staunton (by 'Dorcas', presumably a woman) and on the Rev. John Townsend, formerly of Kingston Independent

Chapel, had been contributed to the *Miscellany*, but it is not recorded that any of the Institution's lectures had been on local history - perhaps Mr. Biden's interests were directed towards Kingston history through the activities of the Institution.

So the influence of the Kingston Literary and Scientific Institution may have been more far-reaching than its founders had envisaged. Many must have had their minds opened to the scientific and industrial developments of the age which may even have been stimulated by such societies. The local firm Jones and Homersham, for example, patented the new oven which used to be called a 'kitchener', one of which was found in an old house in Eden Street, demolished for the second stage of the Eden walk project. Dr. George Taylor's combination of benevolence and practical sense must have been in both respects a sound investment. George Gilbert Scott's building, though finally affected by planning blight, was still earning its keep after nearly 140 years and for most of that time Mr. Biden's book served as the most accessible source of local history for Kingston people. A copy also now costs at least £ 30, whatever that may signify.

Appendix -- The Oxy-hydrogen Microscope {7}

This instrument was virtually a magic lantern with its optical system modified to project microscope slides in place of the standard 3in. x 3in. lantern slides. Whilst a multi-wick oil lamp was just adequate to illuminate the latter, the microscope slides required more intense illumination. This could either be provided by the electric arc or by limelight. Prior to the provision of mains electricity the electric arc required the use of a battery of Daniell cells and was excessively expensive. When an arclight was used to represent the sun at the Paris Opera House in 1837 the cost was equivalent to £ 1.25 per minute. A delightful engraving of an arc microscope is included in the translation of Ganot's *Popular Natural Philosophy*, published in 1878. The illumination used by the Kingston Literary and Scientific Institution was, apparently, limelight. This involved heating a small piece of lime to incandescence by means of an oxy-hydrogen flame. The method was probably identical with that used by my father to illuminate his 'dissolving view lantern' as late as in the 1890s, and by his father before him in the 1870s. The term 'hydrogen' was, almost certainly, used loosely to mean town gas which was popularly called 'carburetted hydrogen'. An old aunt of mine, in her memoirs, describes how my grandfather prepared for a lecture in 1874. The passage is worth quoting in full as it conjures up the period:

'On the evening before the lecture the gas bags had to be filled with oxygen. This meant that big black bags, resembling those used for coal {8} were brought into the breakfast room and placed before the fire. Then our biggest dish was used to mix some preparation composed of black and white powder {9}. This preparation was put into a retort and placed on the fire with a tube attached to the gas bags. It must have been a troublesome process, and the bags did not always fill as they should. It always meant a ruffled and very worried father and a generally disturbed household! We would watch as the bags filled up and got quite big. When they were full they were sent off, together with the boards and lead weights required to compress them, in a horse-drawn cart to the Hall to be ready for the lecture the following day. '

Although my grandfather was a keen photographer, and prepared his own 'wet' plates, he was unable to make his lantern slides and had to hire them from a firm in Newgate Street that had a comprehensive collection covering nearly all scientific, geographical and religious subjects. The heat from an oxy-hydrogen flame was intense and great care had to be taken to avoid cracking the thick condensing lens. Magic lanterns had no fan cooling. The modern projector, with its tungsten-halogen lamp, makes life a lot easier for the lecturer.

1. Copies of *Seeley's Kingston Miscellany* are in **KHC**. [Much of the paper is based on this publication but individual references are not separately footnoted.]

2. For Edward Phillips, see J. Sampson, *Characters of Kingston*, (1974), pp. 8-9.

3. It should be possible to provide a more complete picture of this institution through back numbers of local papers (on microfilm in **KHC**).

4. **Biden**, p. 24. The present whereabouts of the ring is unknown.

5. Private view of the Kingston Heritage Officer.

6. Biden's work was eventually published in 1852.

7. [This postscript was contributed by Mr. D. C. Leeson.]

8. In fact they were made of oiled silk (D.C.L.).

9. Manganese dioxide and potassium chlorate (D.C.L.).

INDEX

INDEX OF PERSONS:

INDEX OF PLACES